James on
Wisdom

How Faith Produces Sensible Living
James 3:13-5:20

Carol Ruvolo

Faith at Work
Studies in the Book of James

DEO VOLENTE
PUBLISHING

Carol Ruvolo, *James on Wisdom*
©1999 by Carol Ruvolo.
Published by Deo Volente Publishing
      P.O. Box 4847
      Los Alamos, NM 87544

Printed in the United States of America.

Scripture taken from the NEW AMERICAN STANDARD BIBLE ®, © Copyright The Lockman Foundation 1960, 1962, 1968, 1971, 1973, 1975, 1977, 1995
Used by permission

Appendices A and B are from *Turning on the Light* by Carol Ruvolo. They are used by permission from P & R Publishing.

ISBN: 0-9658804-2-7

For Carol Meyers,

*whose gentle and quiet spirit
is rooted deep in God's wisdom.*

Table of Contents

Faith at Work
Studies in the Book of James

How to Use this Study Series Effectively

Two books of the Bible have changed my life immeasurably. Paul's letter to the Romans changed the way I think, and James's letter to the twelve tribes dispersed abroad changed the way I live. The two books are very different but entirely consistent. One is filled with skillfully reasoned theology whereas the other bulges with wise practical counsel, but the theology and the counsel never clash. They both form part of the necessary bedrock of faith that enables us to walk worthy of our high calling in Christ Jesus.

As you work through these studies, remember that you are concentrating on one aspect of faith—faith at work—and that these studies, like every other part of Scripture, must be understood within the whole counsel of God.

You also should keep in mind that your time is a gift from God to be used in wise stewardship to accomplish His purposes. Paul advised the Ephesians to make the most of their time because the days are evil, and his words apply to us as well (Ephesians 5:15–17). As you undertake these studies, knowing the following information will help you follow his advice.

Know why you are studying.

The Westminster Shorter Catechism asks the question "What is the chief end of man?" and answers it by saying, "Man's chief end is to glorify God and to enjoy Him forever." (1 Corinthians 10:31; Psalm 73:25–26)[1]

Most of the Christians I know are familiar with that question and answer—even those who have never read the Westminster Confession of Faith or the Catechisms derived from it. Not only are they familiar with the quotation, they like it. They don't argue with it or try to prove it isn't true. Most of them will say they want to live by it. However, most of them don't. The vast majority of Christians I know do not live lives that consistently *glorify God*, and they certainly don't appear to be *enjoying Him forever.*

Why not? If they know they should, and they want to, why don't they? You might be thinking, "Because they're just sinners, that's why!" And that's true—at least it's partially true. They are sinners; however, they are much more than *just* sinners. They are sinners who have been *transformed* by regeneration in Jesus Christ. What they were, they are no longer. Sin no longer is master over them because the Holy Spirit now dwells within them and enables them to obey God. *Every* Christian has the ability to glorify God and enjoy Him forever.

So why don't they? Two reasons come to mind: (1) They know very little of the truth contained in God's Word, and (2) They have never learned how to apply the scriptural truth they do know in everyday life.

Know what you are studying.

These studies were written to help Christians learn how to glorify and enjoy God by living out their transformation in Jesus Christ. They reflect this author's commitment to the Bible as the infallible, inerrant, authoritative, and entirely sufficient Word of God to humanity and her belief that Reformed theology is the clearest and most accurate restatement of God's biblical revelation.

If you are new to Bible study or have doubts about the infallibility, inerrancy, authority, or sufficiency of Scripture, you would benefit greatly from a study such as *A Book Like No Other: What's So Special About the Bible.*[2] You cannot effectively live out your transformation in Jesus Christ without understanding the nature and character of God's unique revelation in Scripture. If you are unfamiliar with Reformed Theology, begin your study by reading Appendix B, "What is the Reformed Faith?"

If you have been studying the Bible for any length of time, you probably are aware of three basic kinds of studies. **Topical studies** present biblical principles regarding a particular *topic*, such as salvation, prayer, love, forgiveness, anger or worry, and they encourage you to grow in your faith by stressing *practical application* of those principles. **Exegetical studies** focus on examining specific portions of Scripture (usually a book or a section of a book) verse by verse, and they concentrate on discovering the meaning of the passage under consideration. **Overview studies** step back and survey sweeping vistas, usually in summary form, with the intent of building a dependable framework for exegetical and topical studies.

All three types of studies should be included in a balanced "Bible study diet" that will be most nourishing for a growing Christian. The studies in the *Faith at Work* series are something of a combination: they examine specific passages of the book of James verse by verse, but they also concentrate on specific topics contained within those verses.

Know what to watch out for.

Exegetical and overview studies are extremely important and nourishing for growing Christians, but they sometimes stop short of *practical application*. Whenever you undertake an exegetical or overview study, be sure you follow through by applying what you have learned to your daily life.

Topical studies are very beneficial because they stimulate believers to grow and mature in their faith; however, they are prone to at least two pitfalls that require alertness on your part: (1) context abuse, and (2) selective proof texting.

Context abuse occurs when a verse or passage is isolated from its surroundings to support a point. For example, how many times have you heard Matthew 18:20 ("For where two or three have gathered together in My name, there I am in their midst") or Matthew 18:19 ("Again I say to you, that if two of you agree on earth about anything that they may ask, it shall be done for them by my Father who is in heaven") referenced in teaching about prayer? Actually, those verses were spoken by Jesus in a discussion of what is commonly known as church discipline, not prayer. Many erroneous doctrines about prayer, however, have been built on this abuse of context.

Selective proof texting occurs when only those verses that seem to support a particular view are cited but those that could be used to refute that view are ignored. You may have heard *selective proof texting* in discussions about whether salvation can be lost or forfeited. Those who say a believer can lose his or her salvation may refer to Galatians 5:4, Hebrews 6: 4-5, Hebrews 10:26–27, and 2 Peter 3:17 but neglect to mention John 10:27–30 or Romans 8:31–39, whereas those who hold the other view will do just the opposite. It's no wonder people say, "You can prove anything you want from the Bible."

Topical studies require you to follow the example of the noble Bereans in Acts 17 by "examining the Scriptures daily, to see whether these things [are] so" (v. 11). Even if you are new to Bible study, you can follow the example of these noble Bereans by developing the habit of (1) always checking the context of isolated verses, and (2) identifying what else the Bible says about the subject you are studying.

Check the context. The Bible originally was not written with chapter and verse designations. Those were added later by translators to make it easier for readers to find specific ideas. Originally, the Bible was written in sentences and paragraphs like any other piece of literature. Remembering this will help you check the context of isolated verses.

Locate the verse in question in your Bible and identify where the *sentence* in which it occurs begins and ends. (Some verses are complete sentences, but most are not.) Now determine where the paragraph containing that sentence begins and ends.[3] Read the entire paragraph to identify the subject being discussed; then ask yourself what the isolated verse says about this subject. If you have time, read the surrounding paragraphs to get an even broader idea of the verse's context. Then go back to the study material and ask yourself if the author used the verse appropriately in relation to its subject matter.

Identify what else Scripture says on the subject. There are several ways to do this. Begin by checking the cross-references in your Bible. These will direct you to other verses where the same words or ideas are discussed.

You also may want to invest in and learn how to use an *exhaustive concordance*. These invaluable reference books list every word in the Bible followed by a list of the verses where each word appears. Many of them also contain a numbering system allowing you to identify and define the original Hebrew and Greek words that were translated into English. These concordances usually are fairly expensive, so be sure to get the most for your money by buying the one that corresponds to the particular translation you use for study. If you need help learning how to use your concordance, ask your pastor, an elder, or other helpful, studious Christians.

A topical Bible like *Nave's* also can be very helpful because it lists references by topics, allowing you to access verses that may discuss the same idea in different words.

Of course, the best way to identify what else the Bible has to say on a particular subject is to become very familiar with the Bible as a whole. This is why following a systematic reading program that structures daily readings to get you through the Bible in a definite time period is so important. Most of these take you "through the Bible in a year," but the time period is not all that important. What is important is that you are reading the entire Bible on a regular basis so that you begin to become familiar with its overall message.

Soon you will find yourself remembering (on your own!) where appropriate cross-references are located. A good Scripture memorization program also helps with this process.

Know with whom you will study.

Ideally, you should pursue both individual study and group study of the Bible. Studying the Bible individually allows the Holy Spirit to deal with you on a very personal basis, whereas group study allows you to learn from other people's insights. If your time is limited, get involved with a group study, but prepare the material individually ahead of time. This way, one set of study materials can do double-duty.

Know how to prepare yourself for study.

Bible study is a serious task that requires careful preparation. It never should be undertaken in a haphazard manner. Take the time to prepare yourself physically, mentally, and spiritually so that you can give your best effort to the Lord.

Physical preparation: Study when you are well-rested and alert. Establish a time and place that is quiet, free of distractions, and conducive to concentration. Get in the habit of taking notes on what you read, and develop a filing system so that you can find those notes later!

Mental preparation: Approach Bible study as you would any task that requires thoughtful effort to do well. Expect it to challenge you and stretch your thinking. Expect it to be difficult at times. And expect it to be extremely rewarding! Spend some time thinking about your daily routine; identify activities that should be limited or eliminated to give you the time you will need to pursue Bible study in a responsible manner. Then schedule blocks of time in your day for study. If you think you can study effectively "whenever the mood hits you," you should think again.

Spiritual preparation: Always begin your study time in prayer. Ask the Lord to reveal sin in your life that needs to be confessed and cleansed, to help you concentrate on His truths, and to illumine your mind to understand what He has written. End your study with a prayer for opportunities to apply what you have learned and wisdom to recognize those opportunities when they occur.

Know whose you are.

Never forget that Bible study equips you *to glorify God and enjoy Him forever.* You glorify God when you live in such a way that those around you can look at you and see an accurate reflection of God's character and nature. You enjoy God when you are fully satisfied and content in His providential ordering of the circumstances of your life. When your life glorifies God and your joy is rooted in His providence, your impact on our fallen world will be tremendous.

I believe John MacArthur expressed these truths very well when he said, "An uncompromising life is characterized by an unashamed boldness that calls us to an uncommon standard. Allow God to do with your life as He pleases, that He might broaden your influence and glorify Himself."

Know how to approach the study questions.

Each chapter in this study is followed by three types of questions: **Review Questions**, **Applying the Word** questions, and **Digging Deeper** questions. The *Review Questions* will help you determine how well you understood the discussion by giving you an opportunity to express its key points in your own words. *Applying the Word* questions encourage you to put your understanding of the chapter's discussion to work in your daily life, and the *Digging Deeper* questions challenge you to pursue further study in certain key areas.

You should be able to find the answers to the *Review Questions* in the chapter's discussion itself, but please resist the temptation to copy words or phrases out of the chapter when you answer these questions. Work at putting these ideas into your own words. When you can do this, you know you have understood what you have read. It might help to ask yourself, "How would I explain this idea to someone else if I didn't have the book with me?"

You should answer at least one of the *Applying the Word* questions. If you do not have time to answer all of them, pray over them and ask the Lord to show you which one(s) *He* wants you to work on. Remember that you are applying what you learned in the chapter to your daily life, so these applications should take some time and thought—and they should be very specific. Avoid vague generalities.

An example illustrating the difference between vague generalities and specific applications might be helpful here. If you were applying the truths found in Philippians 2:3–4 about regarding others as more important than yourself by looking out for their interests, a vague generality would be: "I need to be more helpful and kind to those around me." A specific application would be: "I will call my daughter (who lives in a sorority house on the local college campus) this morning and cheerfully offer to type her term paper while she studies for her final exams. If she accepts my offer, I will do my Saturday chores on Friday instead, leaving Saturday free to help her." Do you see the difference? A specific application answers these questions:

Who?   My daughter

What?   Call and volunteer to type her paper; rearrange my chores

When?   Call this morning; type the paper Saturday; do the chores on Friday

Where? Call from my living room; type the paper at home on my computer or in her room on her computer, whichever is more convenient for her

How?   Cheerfully

A vague generality does not answer these questions. You can make applications in the areas of your thinking, your attitudes, and your behavior. Just remember to be specific! Vague generalities do not help you grow in your faith and do not glorify God. (See Lesson 6 of the *Light for Your Path* study *Turning on the Light* for more information about application.[4])

Digging Deeper questions usually require a significant amount of time and effort to complete. They were designed to provide a challenge for mature Christians who are eager for more advanced study. However, even if you are a new Christian who has done very little Bible study, read these questions and think about them. It will be good for you to be aware of some of these issues so that you can be alert to material you may come across that relates to them.

Remember that you grow by stretching beyond where you are right now, so if one or two of these questions intrigue you, spend some time working on them. And do not hesitate to ask for help from your pastor, elders, or mature Christian friends.

As you work through this study, resist the temptation to compete with other Christians in your group. The purpose of this study is to help you grow in your faith by learning and applying God's truth in your daily life—not to fill up a study book with brilliantly worded answers. If you learn and apply *one element* of God's truth in each chapter, you are consistently moving beyond where you were when you began. Your goal is growth that glorifies God, not impressiveness that glorifies you. Don't ever forget that.

---

[1] *The Shorter Catechism with Scripture Proofs* (Carlisle, Penn: The Banner of Truth Trust), nd. 1.

[2] Carol J. Ruvolo, *A Book Like No Other: What's So Special About the Bible* (Phillipsburg, N.J.: P & R Publishing Co., 1998). Any of the following resources also will help you resolve these issues:

> James M. Boice, *Standing On the Rock*. Grand Rapids: Baker Books, 1994.

> John MacArthur, Jr., *How to Get the Most from God's Word*. Dallas: Word Publishing, 1997.

> Josh McDowell, *Evidence That Demands a Verdict*. San Bernardino, Calif.: Here's Life Publishers, Inc., 1972, 1979.

> B. B. Warfield, *The Inspiration and Authority of the Bible*. Phillipsburg, N.J.: Presbyterian and Reformed Publishing Co., 1948.

[3] Some Bibles are formatted in paragraphs; others use bold type or a figure such as this ¶ to mark paragraphs. Check the introductory material in your Bible to determine how to identify paragraphs.

[4] Carol J. Ruvolo, *Turning on the Light: Discovering the Riches of God's Word* (Phillipsburg, N.J.: P & R Publishing, 1998).

James on Wisdom

James 3:13-5:20

How Faith Produces
Sensible Living

*"Wisdom's ways alone
are ways of pleasantness,
and wisdom's paths alone
are paths of peace."*

J.C. Ryle

Introduction

The Wisdom of Sensible Living

When Paul wrote his New Testament letter to Titus, he described God's purpose for redeeming His chosen: " . . . that He might redeem us from every lawless deed and purify for Himself a people for His own possession, zealous for good deeds" (2:14). His words affirm those of the Westminster divines, who declared the chief end of man to be glorifying God and enjoying Him forever.[1]

If you have worked through the first two books in the *Faith at Work* series, you know that James brings into sharp focus the connection between the good works of redemption and the "chief end" of God's chosen. He emphasizes that "faith without works is dead" (2:17) because faith is revealed by the works that we do (vv. 14–26). James echoes the words of his brother Jesus, who told His disciples, "Let your light shine before men in such a way that they may see your good works, and glorify your Father who is in heaven" (Matthew 5:16). If you read Jesus' words quickly because you've seen them before, please go back and read them again slowly and thoughtfully. When I did that just now, I was struck by the phrase *in such a way*. Apparently we can "let our light shine" in ways that do not glorify God!

In fact, Jesus deals with this very issue a few verses later. In Matthew 6:1, He warns us, "Beware of practicing your righteousness before men *to be noticed by them*" (italics added for emphasis). Obviously Jesus is not saying that we should always practice our righteousness secretly, because if we did, men could not see our good works and glorify God. Rather, Jesus is warning us against practicing our righteousness in such a way as to draw attention to ourselves rather than God. The great Puritan teacher Thomas Manton expressed it this way: "It is one thing to do works that can be seen and another to do works in order that they shall be seen."[2] God is glorified when our shining light of good works illumines His character for those around us to see.

How in the world can we do that effectively? Paul's letter to Titus gives us a concise answer that will serve as our launching pad for this third study of James. Paul says that God's grace has brought us salvation, "instructing us to deny ungodliness and worldly desires and to live sensibly, righteously and godly in the present age" (Titus 2:11–12).

So how in the world do we glorify God with our good works? First of all, we do it *in the world*—or "in the present age." All of creation "naturally" glorifies God—except fallen humanity. (See Romans 1:20–23.) Only those human beings who have been transformed by God's Spirit through the work of salvation (1 Corinthians 2:6–16) have the desire and the ability to glorify Him instead of themselves. One of the reasons He leaves Christians *in the world* after we're saved is to grant us the joyous privilege of living out His created purpose for people.

Secondly, we glorify God with our good works by denying ungodliness and worldly desires. Even though salvation transforms us, it does not eliminate our ability or desire to sin. God left us vulnerable to the snares of the world, the flesh, and the devil so that we would have to depend upon Him to resist temptation. Thus, when we successfully deny ungodliness and worldly desires, He gets the glory— not us. Paul explained it to the Corinthians like this: "But we have this treasure [the testimony of the Gospel] in earthen vessels, that the surpassing greatness of the power may be of God and not from ourselves" (2 Corinthians 4:7).

And thirdly, we glorify God by our good works when we "live sensibly, righteously, and godly." Most of us understand that righteous and godly living involves keeping God's commandments and following the example set for us by Christ and the apostles (1 Peter 1:14–16; 1 John 2:3–6; 1 Corinthians 11:1). But what does Paul mean when he tells us to live *sensibly*? I must admit to being stumped when I asked myself that question a few days ago. So I dusted off my trusty dictionary and looked up the word *sensible*. Here's what I found: "having or showing wisdom or common sense; reasonable; judicious."[3] Sensible living involves living *wisely*, which is what the book of James is all about. .

Many of the commentators I've read label the epistle of James as the "wisdom literature of the New Testament." That's because "wisdom literature" concerns practical issues of life. It takes the great truths of God and applies them to the nitty-gritty of daily events. Even though all of Scripture is useful because of its relevance to real-life situations (2 Timothy 3:16–17; 2 Peter 1:3), a few books of the Bible focus intensely on those practical issues. The wisdom literature of the Old Testament includes Job, Proverbs, and Ecclesiastes;

and the outstanding New Testament example is the book of James.

I'm sure you remember that James was the leader of the first-century Church at the time it was dispersed abroad as a result of severe persecution in Jerusalem (Acts 8:1). The scattered Christians faced many difficulties and trials while living in foreign lands; and James, their compassionate leader, wrote the letter we are studying to encourage them with a reminder of the worth of their faith.

He began "where they were" with a rousing discussion of how Christian faith "works" in trials (James 1:2–25). He reminds his suffering brethren that they have all they need *in their faith* to face any difficulty *in such a way* that God will be glorified and they will have joy. But faith's work in trials is not automatic; it requires activation. That happens when individual Christians prove themselves doers of the Word and not merely hearers. This was the subject of the first book in our study, *James on Trials.*

James then broadens his focus a bit and explains why Christian faith works so well in trials (James 1:26–3:12). The saving faith that redeemed us also transformed us. And redeemed transformation produces good works (such as righteous responses to trials) that glorify God (Isaiah 43:7) and deepen our joy (Psalm 37:3–5) by fulfilling our created purpose (Psalm 35:9, 27–29; Ephesians 2:8–10). We looked at these characteristics of saving faith in the second book in our study, James on Works.

As we embark on the third and final book in our study of James's letter, we will see him broaden his focus still more. In 3:13–5:20, James explains that the characteristics of saving faith that "work" so well in trials "work" equally well in every situation of life. The saving faith that transforms us through Christ's redemption is our source of wisdom for sensible living.

[1] *The Shorter Catechism with Scripture Proofs*. Carlisle, PA: The Banner of Truth Trust, nd, 1.

[2] Thomas Manton, *The Crossway Classic Commentaries: James*. Series editors Alister McGrath and J. I. Packer (Wheaton, Ill.: Crossway Books, 1995), 202.

[3] *The Oxford Dictionary and Thesaurus*, New York: Oxford University Press, American edition (1996), s. v. "sensible."

*"True wisdom shows itself generally
in every part of a man's life
and especially in that wise gentleness
that comes from a proper conception of God
as the Creator
who stands at the beginning of things,
as the Faithful One
who overrules the present,
and as the Judge
who is utterly in control of the future."*

John Blanchard

Chapter One

Wise or Pseudo-Wise?

---

*Who among you is wise and understanding? Let
him show by his good behavior his deeds in the
gentleness of wisdom. But if you have bitter jealousy and selfish ambition in your heart, do not be
arrogant and so lie against the truth. This wisdom
is not that which comes down from above, but is
earthly, natural, demonic. For where jealousy and
selfish ambition exist, there is disorder and every
evil thing. But the wisdom from above is first pure,
then peaceable, gentle, reasonable, full of mercy and
good fruits, unwavering, without hypocrisy. And
the seed whose fruit is righteousness is sown in peace
by those who make peace. (James 3:13–18)*

If you have ever worked at a job that involved han-
dling cash, you have probably been trained to recognize counterfeit currency. Although your training program may have
differed from the one I went through, the goal of them both
was most likely the same: equipping employees to spot phony
money.

Your employer and mine expended valuable company
resources to make sure we developed this particular skill,
and they would not have done so without a good reason.

Failure to recognize counterfeit money almost always results in financial loss to the company. In businesses that handle large volumes of cash, such losses can be substantial if employees aren't good at detecting forgeries. A person or company that accepts a counterfeit bill cannot take it to the Treasury Department and exchange it for a real one. As soon as a counterfeit is unmasked, its owner loses. That's why wise business managers train their employees to distinguish between fake and real money. They know that such an investment will pay off in the long run.

James might have been such a wise businessman in his home town of Nazareth. Since his name comes first in two biblical lists of Jesus' brothers (Matthew 13:55; Mark 6:3), he was probably the eldest of them --- one who would have taken over the family business when Jesus left home to begin His ministry. No doubt, he encountered some counterfeit money.

Being able to spot pseudo-money would have been important to him, and may have helped him see the much greater value of recognizing pseudo-wisdom. James therefore devotes almost half of his letter to equipping his readers to excel in this skill. In 3:13–18, he defines for them the difference between true and false wisdom. And in 4:1–5:20, he fleshes out his description with real-life examples.

Unmasking Deception

Any valuable commodity is subject to counterfeit. Greed and self-interest are not only creative but highly industrious. Every year talented, diligent forgers work overtime to turn out excellent replicas of not only money but also great paintings, fine jewels, and brand-name wearing apparel.

Why do they do it? Why not pour all that time and energy into honest endeavors? Obviously, the forgers believe they have more to gain by trafficking in deception. In their minds, crime not only pays; it pays very well.

Counterfeiting is lucrative because most people fall for it. Forgers count on the fact that you and I cannot distinguish between a real twenty-dollar bill, a real Rembrandt, a real diamond, or even a real pair of Reeboks®, and an imitation. That kind of discernment requires training that most folks don't have. The profit in this kind of crime comes when the deceiver is more skilled in his craft than are the deceived at protecting themselves.

None of us want to suffer the losses that result from falling prey to deception in this material realm. Defending ourselves requires some effort however. Before we can foil an artful forger, we must acquire specialized knowledge of the things in which we are dealing. Wise living involves knowing the difference between the real and the fake.

If this is true in the material world, it is even more true in the spiritual. Being taken in by our enemy, whom Scripture describes as a deceiver (Revelation 12:9) and the father of lies (John 8:44), is a great deal more serious than paying too much for a phony Picasso. Satan works most effectively to disrupt God's purposes by deceiving His saints. He disguises himself as an angel of light and tries to pass off his counterfeit wares as God's genuine articles. One of those wares is counterfeit wisdom. If we don't want to be duped, we must know the difference between it and God's wisdom.

"Who among you is wise and understanding?" James asks his readers. "Let him show by his good behavior his deeds in the gentleness of wisdom" (James 3:13). James wants those who believe that they are wise to examine themselves to see if they have been fooled. True wisdom is an attribute of God (Job 12:13) that He communicates to His people (Proverbs 8:33; Ephesians 5:15). *Gentleness* is a synonym for "humble" or "meek," which when used in regard to a Christian, describes a person whose willing submission to God's authority springs from confident trust in His loving sovereignty.[1]

Therefore, if our "good behavior" reflects both our Father's righteousness and our contentment in His perfect care, we can count ourselves undeceived and genuinely wise. Before we can draw that conclusion, however, we must examine ourselves with the help of God's Holy Spirit (Psalm 139:23–24). Satan's craftiness extends beyond his initial attempts to sell us fake wisdom; he also capitalizes on our propensity for self-justification whenever we seek to analyze our behavior.

That is why James couples wisdom with *understanding*. The Greek word he uses may be applied to someone who is an expert in a particular field. It describes a person who has gained deep knowledge of a subject through observation and study.[2] The ability to distinguish between real and fake wisdom requires such understanding—a deep knowledge of God and of the ways in which He works. J. I. Packer expressed it this way: "Not until we have become humble and teachable, standing in awe of God's holiness and sovereignty . . . acknowledging our own littleness, distrusting our own thoughts, and willing to have our minds turned upside down, can divine wisdom become ours."[3]

This kind of knowledge is available only to those who have been adopted into God's family through redemption in

Christ. All the wisdom of God is embodied in Christ, and our union with Him opens it to us (1 Corinthians 1:30; Colossians 2:2–3). As the Holy Spirit stimulates us to commune with our Father through Bible study and prayer, our understanding of Him grows deeper and stronger (Psalm 119:97–99; 1 Corinthians 2:14–16). And this understanding motivates us to live "in the gentleness of wisdom"—to behave in ways that reflect both our Father's righteousness and our humble submission to His loving authority (Proverbs 3:5–7; Galatians 5:16).

Wisdom from Below

When James wrote his epistle to the dispersed first-century Christians, he knew that many of them were unwise and behaving accordingly. He also knew that although unwise believers cannot lose their salvation (Romans 8:1), neither can they live out God's purpose for their redemption. God adopts children and calls them by His name so that they will display His glory and have fullness of joy (Isaiah 43:7; Psalm 37:4–6; John 15:8–11). Christians who aren't practicing "good deeds in the gentleness of wisdom" can do neither of those things with any degree of effectiveness.

When Christians fail to fulfill God's purpose for them, they play into the hands of the prince of this world. Although Christ's work on the cross broke Satan's power and marked his defeat (John 12:30–33), it did not render believers immune to his crafty devices. Satan's hatred for God is so intense that even Christ's triumph on Calvary hasn't dimmed his desire to derail God's plans. Since we are God's children, we should not be surprised that he targets us.

Since his power to control us is gone, Satan resorts to deception. He can't force us to serve him, but he can delude us into believing that his ways are God's. He does that when he sells us counterfeit wisdom. When he successfully cloaks "bitter jealousy and selfish ambition" (James 3:14) in the guise of God's wisdom, he sows seeds of discord in the Church that obscure God's glory and shackle our joy. Christians who buy Satan's lie end up exchanging good deeds motivated by humble knowledge of God for self-centered activities driven by envy of others and desire for advancement. They operate according to a "wisdom" James tells us "is not . . . from above, but is earthly, natural, demonic" (v. 15).

Many commentators on James have noted the *progression* away from God and His purposes in this description. Earthly wisdom is concerned with the temporal instead of the eternal; natural wisdom is grounded in human potential, not that of the Spirit; and *demonic* wisdom is committed to Satan's agenda rather than God's. James's assessment of counterfeit wisdom aligns itself well with the New Testament's depiction of the three sources of temptation that trouble us as Christians: the world, the flesh, and the devil.

Earthly wisdom pulls us a few steps from God by riveting our attention on the good things in the world. Instead of counting the cost and being willing to sacrifice comfort and ease in pursuit of the Kingdom, we begin to see faith in Christ as our ticket to temporal bliss. Natural wisdom drags us even further from God by assuring us that the temporal success we desire actually depends on our fleshly efforts. We begin to believe we can achieve more in a life apart from God than we can in a life imparted by Him.[4] And demonic wisdom drives us far away from our Father as it drips Satan's venom into our minds: *God doesn't love us. He is just using us.*

We should defend ourselves by working against Him. Do you see how progressive counterfeit wisdom walks hand in hand with progressive temptation?

When we allow Satan to sell us his bill of goods, we give "jealousy and selfish ambition" free rein to incite "disorder and every evil thing" (v. 16) in the body of Christ. And where such things abound, God's glory and our joy will not be able to thrive.

Wisdom from Above

Genuine wisdom is a gift of God. He gives it to us, His children, when He adopts us in Christ. Since "all the treasures of wisdom and knowledge" are hidden in Christ (Colossians 2:3), and our lives as believers are "hidden with Christ in God" (3:3), God's wisdom in Christ is at our disposal. This wisdom is incomprehensible to unbelievers but is "freely given to us" through the work of His Spirit (1 Corinthians 2:6–14). Since we have been blessed with "the mind of Christ" (v. 16), we have no excuse for succumbing to Satan's devices. If we are to live out the purpose for which God redeemed us, our attitudes, actions, and thinking must be controlled by the wisdom that is "from above" (James 3:17).

James says that this kind of wisdom "is first pure, then peaceable, gentle, reasonable, full of mercy and good fruits, unwavering, without hypocrisy" (v. 17)—a masterful description that identifies wisdom's essence as well as its effects. It is "first pure"—that is, pristine and unstained by the world, the flesh, and the devil. In other words, it is thoroughly God's. It comes from God to us through the work of His Son.

The word *then* in James's description marks a transition from wisdom's essence to its effects. As we rely on God's

Spirit to illumine God's Word, His wisdom motivates our soft hearts to live out His purpose for us (Ezekiel 11:19–20; 36:26–27). Our *attitudes* toward the circumstances of life become peaceable, gentle, and reasonable. Our *behavior* begins to be marked by mercy and goodness. And our *thinking* is characterized less and less by hypocrisy and more and more by unwavering devotion to God and His purposes.

What happens when Christians operate according to God's pure wisdom instead of Satan's counterfeit? James says, "the seed whose fruit is righteousness is sown in peace by those who make peace" (v. 18). The syntax of this verse has confounded biblical scholars much brighter than I am, so please forgive my reluctance to unscramble it for you. However, there are two things we can know simply by reading this verse. Those who live in accordance with the pure wisdom of God (1) will reflect God's righteousness to those around them and (2) will be used of God in the role of peacemaker—to make peace between individuals and between God and sinners. Both of these activities glorify God in the world and stimulate joy in our relationship with Him—the very purposes for which He has saved us.

Fulfilling our purpose as God's chosen children requires us to live *wisely*. And as we continue to study the rest of his letter, we'll see James (true to form) describe many practical ways in which we can do that.

---

[1] John MacArthur, Jr., *The MacArthur New Testament Commentary: James.* Chicago: Moody Press, 1998, page 169.

[2] Blanchard, *Truth for Life,* page 201.

[3] *Ibid.*, page 202.

[4] I borrowed the memorable phrasing of this sentence from D. Edmond Hiebert, *James* (Chicago: Moody Press, 1979, 1992), 204.

Review Questions

1. If you have received training designed to equip you to recognize counterfeits, describe this training. Why was it important for you to develop this skill? How does this life experience help you understand the importance of developing skill in recognizing spiritual counterfeits? Explain your answer, using scriptural references to support your understanding. If you have not received this kind of training, how has reading this lesson helped you understand the importance of developing skill in recognizing spiritual counterfeits? Support your answer with Scripture.

2. What is *wisdom*? Consult both a standard dictionary and a biblical or theological dictionary; then write a definition of wisdom in your own words. Be sure to explain the connection between wisdom and understanding.

3. Describe the *alignment* between the progression of temptation (the world, the flesh, and the devil) and the progression of counterfeit wisdom (earthly, natural, and demonic).

4. What is the essence of God's wisdom? What are its effects? How does living in accordance with God's wisdom influence our attitudes, our actions, and our thinking?

5. List the words that James uses in 3:17 to describe God's wisdom. Consider these words, consulting a standard dictionary, a biblical or theological dictionary, and commentaries on James. Then, in your own words, write a clear, concise definition for each of the words that you listed. After you have done so, expand your answer to Review Question 4 to include insights that you may have gained from working on these definitions.

6. What happens when Christians operate by God's pure wisdom instead of by Satan's counterfeit? (Hint: See James 3:18.) What is the significance of what happens?

Applying the Word

1. In his commentary on James, D. Edmond Hiebert highlights the deviousness of Satan's tactics when he says, "Religious zeal or enthusiasm for God and truth is a commendable attitude, but the subtleties of sinful human nature can readily pervert it into bitter antagonism against those who do not express their adherence to God and His truth in the same way we do." (See footnote on page 35; this quotation appears on page 206 of that work.) List one or more specific examples (from your own experience, if possible) that illustrate Hiebert's statement. Then reread James 3:14–16 and explain how these examples reveal Satan's devious tactics at work to "sell" us counterfeit wisdom. Make a plan of action to defend yourself against these devious tactics and share it with someone who loves you enough to hold you accountable.

2. List your favorite television programs and the best movies you
    have seen in the past few months. Then add your favorite books
    to your list. Go back over your list, imagining that Jesus is sit-
    ting by your side. Revise your list until you are comfortable
    with the idea of Jesus participating in these activities with you.
    What does this exercise reveal to you about your sensitivity to
    sin? How will it impact your future use of leisure time?

Digging Deeper

1. Explain *how* reflecting God's righteousness and being used by Him as a peacemaker glorifies God and deepens our joy in our relationship with Him. Consult your Bible concordance and other reliable resources to help you formulate an answer. If you are a relatively new believer, you also may want to work on this question with a more mature Christian.

"For those who would learn God's ways,
humility is the first thing,
humility is the second,
and humility is the third."

Aurelius Augustine

Chapter Two

Genuine Wisdom Is Humble

What is the source of quarrels and conflicts among you? Is not the source your pleasures that wage war in your members? You lust and do not have; so you commit murder. And you are envious and cannot obtain; so you fight and quarrel. You do not have because you do not ask. You ask and do not receive, because you ask with wrong motives, so that you may spend it on your pleasures. You adulteresses, do you not know that friendship with the world is hostility toward God? Therefore whoever wishes to be a friend of the world makes himself an enemy of God. Or do you think that the Scripture speaks to no purpose: "He jealously desires the Spirit which He has made to dwell in us"? But He gives a greater grace. Therefore it says, "God is opposed to the proud, but gives grace to the humble." Submit therefore to God. Resist the devil and he will flee from you. Draw near to God and He will draw near to you. Cleanse your hands, you sinners; and purify your hearts, you double-minded. Be miserable and mourn and weep; let your laughter be turned into

mourning, and your joy to gloom. Humble your-
selves in the presence of the Lord, and He will exalt
you. (James 4:1–10)

When the Apostle Paul wrote his inspired letter to the
believers in Philippi, he admonished them to be humble in
their relationships with each other. He knew that God's pure
genuine wisdom could not be understood and lived out by
proud, arrogant people. Only those who are humble recognize their utter dependence upon the indwelling Spirit to
learn and apply the revealed truths of God. They alone know
that "earthen vessels" (2 Corinthians 4:7) are simply not
strong enough "to live sensibly, righteously and godly in the
present age" (Titus 2:12) without divine help. And they ac-
cede to genuine wisdom's demands that they keep their eyes
fixed firmly on Christ and the pursuit of God's Kingdom.

Consider how Paul expressed this idea to the
Philippians:

If therefore there is any encouragement in Christ, if there
is any consolation of love, if there is any fellowship of
the Spirit, if any affection and compassion, make my
joy complete by being of the same mind, maintaining
the same love, united in spirit, intent on one purpose.
Do nothing from selfishness or empty conceit, but with
humility of mind let each of you regard one another as
more important than himself; do not merely look out for
your own personal interests, but also for the interests of
others. Have this attitude in yourselves which was also
in Christ Jesus (2:1–5).

Paul made similar entreaties in almost every letter he wrote. (For a few examples, see Romans 12:1–3; 1 Corinthians 1:10; Ephesians 4:1–3, Colossians 1:9–10, 3:1–2; and Titus 2:11–14.) He understood as well as James did that genuine wisdom's pure essence requires a heart of humility to make it effective.

Wisdom that is unstained by the world, the flesh, and the devil draws our attention to God and away from ourselves. It teaches us to fulfill our "chief end" by giving God glory in all that we do and by seeking full joy in our relationship with Him. It also unites us in heart, mind, and action with our siblings in Christ.

Whether we read James in the context of Paul, or Paul in the context of James, we find wisdom's heart of humility pumping the life of God's Spirit through the attitudes, actions, and thought patterns of wise believers. Those who are humble of mind, determined to love sacrificially, united in spirit, and intent on the one purpose for which they were saved will show forth the *effects* of God's pure wisdom: "peaceable, gentle, reasonable, full of mercy and good fruits, unwavering, without hypocrisy" (James 3:17).

James underscores humility's role in genuine wisdom by prefacing his practical illustrations with a clear warning against trading humble submission to Christ and God's purposes for a proud, arrogant focus on ourselves and the world.

Wrong Motives

Christians who use Scripture to counsel troubled brothers and sisters know that at the root of most (if not all) unrighteous behavior lies a focus on self and/or the world instead of on God. James surely became an experienced and capable "biblical counselor" during his tenure as leader of the church in Jerusalem.

"What is the source of quarrels and conflicts among you?" he asks and then offers this keen diagnosis: "Is not the source your pleasures that wage war in your members?" (James 4:1). Did you notice that James wasn't as concerned with the quarrels and conflicts themselves as he was with their origin?

Believers in Christ frequently disagree with each other. When we do, we tend to concentrate *on the disagreement itself* by seeking to determine who's right and who's wrong. Although that effort may prove very valuable (especially for those who affirm Scripture's inerrant authority), the disagreement itself may not be the real issue. When disagreements escalate into "quarrels and conflicts," they become symptomatic of a much deeper problem. As James so aptly stated, they reflect an unrighteous self-centered focus on our "pleasures that wage war in [our] members"—in other words, a lack of humility.

Most of us find it remarkably easy to overlook this deeper problem in the heat of an argument, but wise gifted teachers down through the ages have cautioned us not to do so. In Psalm 8, David captured the soul of humility in his eloquent depiction of our complete dependence upon our Creator. Because we are by nature dependent beings, self-absorption is always counterproductive to God's purposes for us. That's why the prophet Isaiah reminds us that God dwells with "the contrite and lowly of spirit" (57:15), and Micah records God's requirement that we walk humbly with Him (6:8). Paul sums up humility well when he tells us to boast in the Lord (1 Corinthians 10:31; 2 Corinthians 10:17), not in ourselves (1 Corinthians 1:26–29) or in other people (3:18–21).

John Chrysostom, an early Church father, identified humility as "the foundation of our philosophy." Augustine said it was the first, second and third precept of the Christian religion. Thomas à Kempis and Bernard declared that the imitation of Christ is impossible without it. And Martin Luther warned against one of pride's cleverest disguises—"seeking to excel in humility"—when he said, "Unless a man is always humble, distrustful of himself, always fears his own understanding . . . passions . . . will, he will be unable to stand for long without offense. Truth will pass him by."[1]

John Calvin, characteristically, identified humility as a necessary means of exalting God's sovereignty. "Our humility is His loftiness," he said. Without it, we cannot practice self-denial nor lay aside self-confidence and self-will in recognition of our dependence upon Him for everything.[2]

These men understood that we must be humble before we can apply the wisdom of God in our lives. When we focus on ourselves and the world, we are not intent upon God and the pursuit of His kingdom. Such pride constitutes spiritual adultery (James 4:4) because it transfers to illegitimate objects the committed devotion we owe to God alone. Spiritual adultery can't be hidden for long; it inevitably bears fruit that testifies of its lineage.

The first fruits of pride are usually born in our relationships with each other. The "unity of the Spirit," which we are instructed to "preserve . . . in the bond of peace" (Ephesians 4:3) is easily shattered by quarrels and conflicts. James says, "You lust and do not have; so you commit murder. And you are envious and cannot obtain; so you fight and quarrel" (v. 2). Preoccupation with self-seeking desire (lust) and self-exalting activities (envy) unleashes a destructive barrage of interpersonal sins, ranging from quarreling to murder, that devastate our unified witness. When that witness shatters, so does our ability to glorify God and enjoy Him intensely.

James indicates that spiritual adultery also bears bitter fruit in our relationship with our Father because of its harmful impact upon our prayers. Those who pray best are the most humble. They approach God's throne in awe of His sovereign majesty. They recognize their dependence upon Him for every aspect of being and acknowledge their gratitude for His mercy and grace. They affirm His exclusive right to their devotion, ask His forgiveness for their sins against Him, and claim His promises to meet all their needs in His service. (See Matthew 6:9–13.) Such humble prayers glorify God (John 14:13–15) and fill up our joy (John 16:24) because they focus our attention on Him instead of on ourselves. God-focused Christians pray very well (1 John 5:13–15); tragically, self-focused Christians do not.

When God's children lose sight of their dependence upon Him, they may simply stop praying. And as their sinful self-confidence quenches their prayers, it also slams shut the door on God's storehouse of blessing. James says these Christians don't have because they don't ask (James 4:2). When God's children retain a sense of their dependence on Him but couple it with consuming worldly desires, they may begin to view God as their "source" of earthly bliss. These Christians invariably continue to pray, but "with wrong motives" to "spend it on [their] pleasures." For that reason, James explains, when they ask, they will not receive (4:3).

Lack of humility is serious business. It negates both the understanding and practice of genuine wisdom. It has that effect because it is spiritual adultery as well as "friendship with the world,"—and "whoever wishes to be a friend of the world makes himself an enemy of God" (4:4).

Those who love God (as you and I do!) do not desire to make themselves His enemies. Thus, we want to be humble. However we have been warned that "pursuing humility" can be counterproductive. As Martin Luther has indicated, as soon as we say to ourselves *I believe I am humble,* we have fallen into pride's snare. So how can we "humble ourselves" as the Bible commands? It seems clear to me that we can't. Our only recourse is to throw ourselves on God's mercy and to rely on His "greater grace."

Greater Grace

Grace cannot be received by someone who is proud. That's because grace, by definition, is *"unmerited favor,"* and the proud person believes that the favor is *merited*. God's gift of grace is reserved for the humble because they alone know that they don't deserve it.

Most of us think of grace as being received at the time of salvation (Ephesians 2:8–9; Titus 3:4–7), but we tend to forget that it doesn't stop there. And such forgetfulness is not very wise. If we are to live sensibly in the present age, we must remember the equipping effects of the grace of salvation. As God's saving grace places us in His family, it transforms and sustains us to live out the purpose for which He redeemed us.[3]

If we bear that truth in mind, we won't fall prey to the counterfeit wisdom that misdefines grace as the freedom to live "however we choose." D. Edmond Hiebert, in his commentary on James, emphasizes that God's promise of grace was never intended to encourage His people to think lightly of sin.[4] Our Father is jealous of our devotion (James 4:5)[5] and demands from us wholehearted loyalty (2 Corinthians 5:14–15). Sin draws our attention from Him to ourselves while it splits our allegiance between His pursuits and the world's. Therefore, the grace that He gives us cannot be rightly seen as a license to sin. Rather, as one of my favorite Bible teachers has said, "Grace does not mean that we have permission to do as we please; it means we have the power to do what pleases God."

Paul dealt with this issue decisively in his epistle to the Christians in Rome. Although "where sin increased, grace abounded all the more" (Romans 5:20), we are *not* (definitely, emphatically not) "to continue in sin that grace might increase" (6:1–2). That's because we have died to sin (v. 2) and have been united with Christ (v. 5). God's saving grace has freed us from sin's power (vv. 6, 14), has enslaved us to God (v. 22), and sustains us as we pursue righteousness (vv. 12–13) by obeying God from the heart (v. 17).

The transforming grace that enables us to live out God's purpose for our salvation is what James calls "greater grace." It is grace that does more than confirm our reservations in heaven. It is the grace that we find at God's merciful throne when we look to His help in our time of need (Hebrews 4:16). It is the grace that convicts us by the work of the Spirit when we succumb to the allure of the world, the flesh, and the devil—then draws us to confess and seek His cleansing forgiveness. It is the grace that removes our transgressions from us "as far as the east is from the west" (Psalm 103:12–13) and gives us innumerable chances to start over again (1 John 1:9). And it is the grace that teaches us how to live for God's glory in inexpressible joy (Psalm 32:8–11).

Humble Yourselves

Thomas Manton likened knowing sound doctrine to drawing a bow—and applying that knowledge to hitting the target. He then went on to comment that many Christians are "wise" in the generalities of doctrine, but foolish in actual practice.[6] James doesn't want his beloved readers to be included in Manton's description. Therefore he extends his discussion of humility beyond knowing doctrine to applying it in our lives.

"Don't be foolishly satisfied with the mere knowledge of what humility is," he says in effect. "Be truly wise by putting that knowledge to work—by humbling yourselves." James emphasizes five aspects of *humbling ourselves*: (1) submission to God, (2) resisting the devil, (3) drawing near to God, (4) repenting of sin, and (5) trusting God. Did you notice that three of the five fix our attention directly on God while the other two must be done in reference to Him? That coincides perfectly with the doctrinal teaching of Scripture regarding the practice of humility: It rests upon understanding our utter dependence on God. James now urges us to live wisely by acting in ways that reflect that understanding.

Humbling ourselves requires, first of all, an *attitude* of submission to God. An attitude is a settled opinion or way of thinking. Attitudes develop over time as a result of thought-fully considering the realities of life. They are more mental than emotional and more persistent than temporary. I like to think of them as the "colored glasses" through which we view life.

An attitude of submission acknowledges and yields willingly to rightful authority. Submissive Christians delight to work under God instead of against Him. They are not af-ter God's job because they know they can't do it. They re-joice in the security they find in His sovereignty and appre-ciate being chosen to participate in His work. They know that they are creatures dependent on their Creator for every facet of life. If we are among them, we have the mindset we need to practice humility.

This attitude of submission must completely encom-pass the four actions we take to "humble ourselves"—resist-ing the devil, drawing near to God, repenting of sin, and trust-ing our Father. We must recognize our fallen inability to do any of these without the equipping power of His Holy Spirit.

Resisting Satan effectively certainly demands com-plete dependence on God. Peter describes Satan as a "roar-ing lion" who prowls about "seeking someone to devour" (1 Peter 5:8). But he also affirms that Satan is no match for the Christian who is submitted to God. "But resist him, firm in your faith," Peter says (v. 9), *after* you have "[cast] all your anxiety upon Him, because He cares for you" (v. 7) and *know-ing* that "the God of all grace . . . will Himself perfect, con-firm, strengthen and establish you" (v. 10).

What a comfort to know that we don't have to face Satan alone, and how foolish we are when we try to do so!

Wisdom dictates that we follow the archangel Michael's example. Jude tells us "when he [Michael] disputed with the devil and argued about the body of Moses, [he] did not dare pronounce against him a railing judgment, but said, 'The Lord rebuke you'" (v. 9). An attitude of submission reminds us of our childlike reliance upon the Mighty One who created Satan, allowed him to fall, and defeated him soundly at Calvary (John 12:30–33).

That same attitude also enables us to draw near to God. Scripture tells us that God is "near to the brokenhearted" (Psalm 34:18) , will not despise "a broken and contrite spirit" (51:17). And that although heaven is His throne and the earth His footstool, He will look to "him who is humble and contrite of spirit, and who trembles at [His] word" (Isaiah 66:1–2).

Without a submissive spirit, our fallen propensity for self-justification will interfere with repentance of our sin. We must depend upon God, who is supremely able and willing to search our hearts, reveal our sin to us, and help us confess it (Psalm 19:12–14; 139:23–24; 1 Corinthians 4:3–4).

Finally, an attitude of submission encourages us to trust God. Inherent dependence walks hand in hand with necessary reliance. And when the One to whom we must look for protection and care is all–powerful, righteous, and good, we quickly learn to trust Him completely. Thus, James's command, "Humble yourselves in the presence of the Lord" (James 4:10), is not an ominous threat but a thrilling privilege. Submission has taught us that God keeps His promises; therefore, we know (definitely, emphatically *know*) that He will exalt us.

[1] The information in this paragraph, as well as the quotation from Martin Luther, was cited in R. E. O. White, "Humility," in *Evangelical Dictionary of Theology,* ed. Walter A. Elwell (Grand Rapids: Baker Book House, 1984), page 537.

[2] John T. McNeill, editor, *The Library of Christian Classics,* Volumes XX and XXI—*Calvin: Institutes of the Christian Religion,* translated by Ford Lewis Battles (Philadelphia: The Westminster Press, 1960), II. ii. 11; III. vii. 4, xii. 6–7.

[3] For a most helpful discussion of this important truth, see Jerry Bridges, *Transforming Grace: Living Confidently In God's Unfailing Love.* Colorado Springs: NavPress, 1991.

[4] D. Edmond Hiebert, *James* (Chicago: Moody Press, 1979, 1992), 235. Original title, *The Epistle of James.*

[5] This verse is another "interpretive nightmare" which has generated much lively discussion among commentators on James. It seems fairly obvious from the context that aside from the questions that the verse raises, the verse does indicate that God expects and requires exclusive devotion and loyalty from His children.

[6] Thomas Manton, *The Crossway Classic Commentaries: James,* series editors Alister McGrath and J. I. Packer (Wheaton, Ill.: Crossway Books, 1995), 245.

Review Questions

1. Read Romans 12:1–16; Ephesians 4:1–16; Philippians 2:1–13; Colossians 1:9–14; 3:1–2; and Titus 2:11–14. Then reread James 3:13–4:10. Use the truths of God found in these verses to help you explain why genuine wisdom (which is essentially *pure* because it is from God) requires a *heart of humility* to make it effective.

2. Describe the "deeper problem" that was producing quarrels and conflicts among James's readers. Give several examples of cautions that wise and gifted teachers, down through the ages, have given against overlooking this problem when we disagree with each other. Then explain why we would be wise to heed their advice.

3. Describe the "fruit" born by prideful self-absorption (which James equates with spiritual adultery) both in our relationships with each other and in our relationship with our Father. How does this fruit influence the way we live out God's purpose for us?

4. Explain D. Edmond Hiebert's insightful, true statement that God's promise of grace was never intended to encourage his people to think lightly of sin. (Be sure to include a description of how God's grace does more than confirm our reservations in heaven.)

5. List and briefly describe the five aspects of "humbling ourselves" that James emphasizes in 4:7–10. Explain the relationship between the first aspect he mentions, which is an attitude,
   to the other four, which are actions.

6. Look up *humility* and/or *humble* in a biblical dictionary, or consult reliable commentaries on James 4:1–10 regarding these
   words. Based upon what you have learned from those sources
   and from this lesson, write a definition of *humility* in your own
   words. Then explain why humility is a necessary ingredient in
   wise Christian living.

Applying the Word

1. Describe your last disagreement with another Christian. How did you handle the situation? Describe your attitudes, thoughts, and actions as well as the actions of the other believer. (You cannot describe his or her attitudes and thoughts accurately, of course.) Did the disagreement escalate into a quarrel or a conflict? If so, describe the circumstances surrounding the escalation. Was the disagreement resolved? If so, how? Considering what you have learned in this lesson, do you believe that a lack of humility *on your part* may have played a role in the disagreement itself or its escalation into a quarrel or conflict? If so, what specific changes do you need to make in your attitudes, thoughts, and actions that will help you handle future disagreements with other Christians in ways that will glorify God and increase your joy in your relationship with Him?

2. Let's not be foolishly satisfied with a mere knowledge of what humility is. Let's be truly wise by putting that knowledge to work by humbling ourselves! Answer the following questions honestly and specifically.

Are there areas of your life in which you are resisting (or actively rebelling against) God's rightful authority over you? If so, describe the areas and your attitude. What steps must you take to develop an attitude of submission to God in these areas? Make a specific plan to help you develop this attitude.

Do you believe that Satan is currently "seeking to devour you" in some particular way? If so, how can you benefit from the example of the archangel Michael in Jude 9 as you work at resisting him?

Are some of your current activities preventing you from drawing near to God? If so, with what specific activities will you replace them?

Are you harboring unconfessed sin? If so, use Psalm 19:12–14, Psalm 139:23–24, and 1 John 1:9 to help you seek God's cleansing forgiveness immediately.

When was the last time you meditated on God's power, righteousness, and goodness as a means of strengthening your trust in Him? If it has been more than a week, use a concordance to locate Scripture passages describing these attributes of God; then devote an hour or more to thoughtful consideration of how these aspects of His nature encourage submission and trust on your part.

Digging Deeper

1. Explain why grace is not "permission to do as we please" but, rather, "having the power to do what pleases God." Support your explanation with Scripture.

2. Relate James's description of the effects of God's wisdom (3:17) with the aspects of humbling ourselves that he outlines in 4:7–10 by answering the following questions:

   How does an attitude of submission foster the wise *attitudes* of peaceableness, gentleness, and reasonableness?

How does resisting Satan, drawing near to God, repenting of sin, and trusting God generate wise actions that are full of mercy and good fruits?

How do these four activities stimulate wise *thinking* that is characterized less and less by hypocrisy and more and more by unwavering devotion to God and His purposes?

*"To believe actively that our heavenly Father
constantly spreads around us
the providential circumstances
that work for our present good
and our everlasting well-being,
brings to the soul a veritable benediction....
Our insistence on seeing ahead is natural enough,
but it is a real hindrance to our spiritual progress.
God has charged Himself with full responsibility
for our eternal happiness
and stands ready to take over the
management of our lives
the moment we turn in faith to Him."*

A.W. Tozer

Chapter Three

Genuine Wisdom Submits to God

Do not speak against one another, brethren. He who speaks against a brother, or judges his brother, speaks against the law, and judges the law; but if you judge the law, you are not a doer of the law, but a judge of it. There is only one Lawgiver and Judge, the One who is able to save and to destroy; but who are you who judge your neighbor? Come now, you who say, "Today or tomorrow, we shall go to such and such a city, and spend a year there and engage in business and make a profit." Yet you do not know what your life will be like tomorrow. You are just a vapor that appears for a little while and then vanishes away. Instead, you ought to say, "If the Lord wills, we shall live and also do this or that." But as it is, you boast in your arrogance; all such boasting is evil. Therefore, to one who knows the right thing to do, and does not do it, to him it is sin. (James 4:11–17)

All of us seem to have a built-in aversion to the idea of submission. Just mention the word in a room full of women and you'll see what I mean! But we ladies haven't cornered the market on that reaction. Don't you know a few men who would rather spend six hours lost than ask for directions?

How many times has a toddler (male or female) looked you right in the eye while proceeding to do exactly what you had forbidden? Don't most of us (men and women alike) drive five miles over the speed limit as a matter of habit? Didn't we persistently come home ten minutes past curfew when we were teenagers?

Aversion to submission isn't gender specific. Rather it is specific to our fallen sin nature. The Westminster Shorter Catechism defines *sin* as "any want of conformity unto, or transgression of, the law of God" (Q/A 14). In practical terms, we could boil that down to "submission aversion." Sins of omission (want of conformity unto the law of God) and sins of commission (transgression of the law of God) reflect an attitude of defiance against rightful authority, which is rooted in pride.

James tells us that such an attitude is extremely unwise. Rightful authority, in all of its forms, has been instituted by God for His own glory and, consequently, for the good of His people. God created us as dependent beings subject to authority because that condition enhances His glory and fills up our joy. Pastor-teacher John Piper expressed it like this: "All the omnipotent energy that drives the heart of God to pursue His own glory, also drives Him to satisfy the hearts of those who seek their joy in Him."[1]

Satan roots sin in pride to disrupt both of those purposes. He knows, from personal experience (Isaiah 14:12–17), that creatures absorbed with themselves do not seek to fulfill God's purposes for them. He delights in luring God's children away from pursuit of the Kingdom with provocative calls to arrogant self-reliance.

In Chapter Two, we saw how James exhorted his readers to wisely acknowledge their dependence on God, humble themselves in His presence, and expect opposition from Satan (James 4:1–10). In this chapter, we will concentrate on his description of three practical areas in which we must apply that exhortation (vv. 11–17). As Christians, we must practice submission to God in (1) the ways in which we speak about and to others, (2) the ways in which we plan our activities, and (3) the ways in which we respond to God's truth in general.

Critical Speech Judges God's Law

James has already exhorted his readers at length regarding the importance of controlling their tongues (3:1–12). Thus at this point in his discussion of wisdom, he simply reminds us that our speech indicates the state of our hearts. A proud, arrogant spirit finds it remarkably easy to "speak against" others (v. 11). It expresses itself in biting criticism, scathing condemnation, and careless gossip. It does not hesitate to falsely accuse, exaggerate faults, malign motives, rehash mistakes, and assassinate character. It gives no thought to the edification of others because its attention is focused fully on itself. Those who hold lofty views of themselves must, of necessity, look down on others. And no one should be surprised when they speak accordingly.

Psalm 101:5 associates slander with a haughty look and an arrogant heart. It also affirms that God *will not endure* those who are characterized by such behavior and attitudes. James doesn't pull any punches when he explains God's intransigence: "He who speaks against a brother, or judges his brother, speaks against the law, and judges the law; but if you judge the law, you are not a doer of the law, but a judge of it. There is only one Lawgiver and Judge, the One who is able to save and to destroy; but who are you to judge your neighbor?" (vv. 11–12).

Early in his letter, James admonished his readers to be doers of God's law and not merely hearers (1:22). At that point he was emphasizing our need to practice God's truth to overcome trials, but now he proceeds to broaden that emphasis. Doing God's law "works" well in trials because it is the key to wise living in general.

God did not give us His law in the language of suggestion. Nowhere in Scripture does He ask our opinion of His commandments. Since God alone has full, perfect knowledge of His plans and purposes, He does not give us the right to pass judgment on His proclamations. When we read God's law and *decide* not to obey it, we usurp a prerogative God has reserved for Himself. We arrogantly assert our fallen opinion that a particular law is not worth obeying. We exalt ourselves above God, discard the "wisdom from above" (James 3:17) in favor of that which is "earthly, natural, demonic" (v. 15), and clear the way for jealousy, selfish ambition, disorder, and every evil thing to disrupt God's family (v. 16).

Naturally, exchanging God's truth for the ways of the world profoundly affects the ways in which we speak about and to others. When our attitudes are so arrogant as to judge God and His law, we will think nothing of judging our brothers and sisters as well. The Greek word translated *judge* in verse 11 (*krino*) means "to sit in judgment" or "to pass judgment," and carries the idea of condemnation.[2] It describes another activity that God has wisely and rightly reserved for

Himself. We fallen humans are simply not qualified to judge others because we lack full knowledge and perfect integrity. God's law commands us to love each other instead. James had undoubtedly heard his brother Jesus declare that "the whole Law and the Prophets" depend upon these two commandments: "You shall love the Lord your God with all your heart, and with all your soul, and with all your mind . . . [and] love your neighbor as yourself" (Matthew 22:37–39). James surely understood that those who love God will not worship other gods, make graven images, take His Name in vain, nor profane His Sabbath—and that those who love their neighbors will not murder them, lie to them, steal from them, commit adultery against them, covet their possessions, nor dishonor their closest neighbors, their parents. (See Exodus 20:1–17.)

That is why James told his readers to govern their human relationships by God's "royal law" (2:8). When we do that, we will not speak *against* others but rather for the purpose of edification (Ephesians 4:29). Speech that edifies others does not condemn them. Rather it calls them to pursue their highest interests by submitting themselves to God's commandments.

Many Christians misunderstand the nature and purpose of edification, thinking that it must always be pleasant and easy to hear. But, realistically, that is simply not true. Words that edify not only compliment and commend those who do well, but they also gently rebuke and exhort those who commit sin or fail to walk worthy of their high calling in Christ. Thus, those who interpret "Do not judge your brother" to mean "Never reprove or correct" are just as unloving as those who condemn. Paul, in his classic definition of love, tells us that it "does not rejoice in unrighteousness, but rejoices with the truth" (1 Corinthians 13:6). Paul knew that evaluating the behavior of others in light of God's truth and restoring those "caught in any trespass . . . *in a spirit of gentleness*" (Galatians 6:1; italics added for emphasis) is not condemnation, but edification motivated by love.

Wise Christians submit to the "one Lawgiver and Judge" in their interactions with others. They acknowledge His sovereign right to judge His creatures' behavior, and they accept His standard of Scripture as the sole criteria for the edification of others. These wise Christians aren't hard to recognize: Their manner of speech reflects the state of their hearts.

Independence in Planning Is Practical Atheism

William Ernest Henley has eloquently captured the meaning of the phrase *practical atheism* in his famous poem "Invictus."[3]

> *Out of the night that covers me,*
> *Black as the Pit from pole to pole*
> *I thank whatever gods may be*
> *For my unconquerable soul.*

> *In the fell clutch of circumstance*
> *I have not winced nor cried aloud.*
> *Under the bludgeonings of chance*
> *My head is bloody, but unbowed.*
> *Beyond this place of wrath and tears*

Looms by the Horror of the shade,
And yet the menace of the years
Finds, and shall find me unafraid.

It matters not how strait the gate,
How charged with punishments the scroll,
I am the master of my fate;
I am the captain of my soul.

Simon J. Kistemaker describes practical atheism much more succinctly as living as if God does not exist. And then he goes on to say that practical atheism is one of *the most common sins committed by Christians*.[4] Does that statement surprise you—perhaps even shock you? If so, you were probably jarred by the use of the word *"atheism"* in regard to a believer. It definitely caught your attention! Maybe it even forced you to stop and think. Could that be why so many good teachers use the phrase *practical atheism* to depict James's warning to the independently minded?

"Come now," James says to his readers, "you who say, 'Today or tomorrow, we shall go to such and such a city, and spend a year there and engage in business and make a profit.' Yet you do not know what your life will be like tomorrow. You are just a vapor that appears for a little while and then vanishes away. Instead you ought to say, 'If the Lord wills, we shall live and also do this or that'" (4:13–15).

Was James anti-business? or anti–profit? or anti–diligence? No, he was not. We must interpret his words in the context in which he was writing. James wants his readers to live *wisely* as Christians. He knows we can't do that by pursuing our daily activities as if God doesn't exist. Such arrogance is unwise because it fails to glorify God and fill up our joy. John Blanchard, in his book *Truth for Life*, explains it this way: "Now of course James was not suggesting that they just sit back and do nothing. He was not condemning their business but their boasting; not their industry but their independence; not their acumen but their arrogance. What he is telling them is that the right attitude to life is to recognize that God is in sovereign control of it all, and that it should be yielded in humble submission to his divine will."[5]

Wise Christians do more than pay lip service to God's absolute sovereignty; they order their lives in complete dependence upon it. When they close their Bibles to go do their chores, they don't forget that God alone gives "life and breath" to all things (Acts 17:25). They face each new day's assortment of joys, troubles, and challenges secure in the knowledge that He is the reason they "live and move and exist" (Acts17: 28). They lean on His Spirit for guidance in all their endeavors and delight to be used as His means to accomplish His purposes. They work hard by day and sleep well by night because they have learned to rely completely on God's all-sufficient grace, which is abundant for every good deed (2 Corinthians 9:8). They do not use God's sovereign provision as a justification for sloth or for lack of planning. Rather, in the paraphrased words of D. Edmond Hiebert, they commit all to Him and continue according to plan "under the encouraging sense of God's guidance and sustaining grace."[6]

Wise Christians are those who have rightly chosen to walk humbly with God instead of to walk proudly without Him (Deuteronomy 10:12–13; Micah 6:8). They glorify God by their acknowledged dependence upon Him and fill up their joy in their unfailing confidence in His perfect care. Their lives reveal the reality of the faith at work in them.

Knowing Without Doing Is Sin

James skillfully summarizes the wisdom of submission when he says to his readers, "But as it is, you boast in your arrogance; all such boasting is evil. Therefore, to one who knows the right thing to do, and does not do it, to him it is sin" (4:16–17). His words serve to remind us again that every sin in the book is rooted in pride.

Whenever we yield to the temptation to think more highly of ourselves than we ought, submission to God slips inexorably toward arrogant independence. When we allow ourselves to lose sight of our utter dependence on God, our allegiance soon shifts from pursuit of His Kingdom to self-exaltation.

We may be running well—focused on God, taking every thought captive to Christ, seeking the Spirit's enablement to serve Him effectively, and expressing our gratitude for successes in ministry. Our confidence builds, and our guard drops a little. We forget the wise words of our brother Paul, "Therefore let him who thinks he stands take heed lest he fall" (1 Corinthians 10:12), and open a chink in our spiritual armor. Satan, our vigilant enemy, quickly attacks at the vulnerable spot by slyly complimenting our personal achievements, to which we are apt to respond, *Why, thank you. I did do rather well in that ministry effort, didn't I?* Thus begins our destructive descent of the slippery slope of "arrogant independence."

As our slide gains momentum, we make easier targets. Satan does not have to work nearly so hard to keep us rolling downhill once we've started moving. That's why every Christian should memorize Paul's warning in 1Corinthians 10:12 along with his words of encouragement in the verse that follows: "No temptation has overtaken you but such as is common to man; and God is faithful, who will not allow you to be tempted beyond what you are able, but with the temptation will provide the way of escape also, that you may be able to endure it."

Wise Christians know that their best defense against the temptations of the world, the flesh, and the devil is to maintain a good grip on the truth of God's Word. If we consistently learn it and do it, we will not slip so often. And when we do drop our guard and find ourselves falling, we can use God's Word, stored in our hearts, as an emergency handhold. All we need do to arrest our descent is reach out and grasp a well-placed memory verse.

Since our enemy knows that our deadliest weapon against him is Scripture, he works hard to drive wedges between it and us. If we want to live wisely in the present age, we must rely on God's truth as our means of *recognizing* (taking heed lest we fall) and *defeating* (laying hold of God's way of escape) the temptation of pride—particularly when it comes as an assault on the Bible itself.

When Satan appeals to our intellect by insisting that Scripture has no inherent authority, is unreliable, and hardly sufficient for "New Millennium" Christians, we must recall that he is the father of lies, who delights in discrediting truth (John 8:44–45). When he flatters us by suggesting that we are fully capable of running our lives without the "crutch" of a dusty old book, we must remember the heartbreaking examples of others he has deceived down through the ages. (See Genesis 3:1–5 and 2 Samuel 11–12 for two clear examples.) When he assures us that we are thoroughly qualified to pass judgment on Scripture by accepting some passages and discarding others, we must follow Christ's example of righteous humility and respond that our lives depend upon "every word that proceeds out of the mouth of God" (Matthew 4:4; italics added for emphasis).

Satan's assaults on God's Word are carefully calculated to separate our behavior from what we know from Scripture is "the right thing to do" (James 4:17). He does that by appealing to our built-in aversion to being submissive. Every time he persuades us to *judge* Scripture instead of *obey* it, he persuades us to sin. And when we sin, we cease to pursue our chief end as God's children. We then must repent and confess to get back on track (1 John 1:9).

Christians do not have to succumb to Satan's devices. God gives us everything that we need for life and godliness (2 Peter 1:3–4) in His Word and His Spirit (Ephesians 5:18ff; Colossians 3:16ff). We *have been equipped* to glorify God and enjoy Him forever by living sensibly, righteously, and godly in the present age. But using that equipment effectively requires our complete dependence on Him. Humble submission to God is thus the key to wise living—which, by the way, also opens the door to the *righteous* exaltation that God Himself has prepared for us (James 4:10; 1 Peter 5:6).

[1] John Piper, *Desiring God: Meditations of a Christian Hedonist* (Sisters, Ore.: Multnomah Books, 1986, 1996), 53.

[2] W. E. Vine, Merrill F. Unger, and William White Jr., *Vine's Expository Dictionary of Biblical Words,* s.v. "Judge" (Nashville, Tenn.: Thomas Nelson Publishers, 1985).

[3] Quoted in John MacArthur Jr., *The MacArthur New Testament Commentary: James* (Chicago: Moody Press, 1998), 234.

[4] Simon J. Kistemaker, *New Testament Commentary: Exposition of James, Epistles of John, Peter, and Jude* (Grand Rapids: Baker Books, 1996), 146. Originally published in separate volumes.

[5] John Blanchard, *Truth For Life: A Devotional Commentary on the Epistle of James* (Durham, England: Evangelical Press, 1986), 315.

[6] D. Edmond Hiebert, *James* (Chicago: Moody Press, 1979, 1992), 254.

Review Questions

1. Practically speaking, how does the Westminster Shorter Catechism's definition of sin boil down to "submission aversion"? Read James 4:1–17 in the light of Proverbs 3:1–25, Isaiah 14:12–16, Romans 8:31–39, and 1 Peter 5:6–11; then use what you learn from your reading to explain why submission aversion is extremely unwise.

2. List the three *practical areas* James describes in which we must apply his exhortations in 4:1–10 to acknowledge our dependence on God, humble ourselves in His presence, and expect opposition from Satan. Do you think that James has "covered the bases" of Christian submission by using these particular examples? In other words, can you think of any areas of Christian submission that are not covered by his discussion of these three areas?

3. Describe several ways in which a proud, arrogant spirit can be revealed in our speech. What does Psalm 101:5 say about those with proud, arrogant spirits? What light does James shed on God's attitude toward the arrogant in 4:11–12?

4. What effect does exchanging God's truth for the ways of the world have upon the ways in which we speak about and to others? What effect does obeying God's command to love each other have upon our speech? (In your answer, be sure to explain the difference between condemnation and edification.)

5. What is "practical atheism"? Can you think of some ways in which you have been (or are) guilty of committing this sin? How should we guard against committing this sin?

6. How will memorizing 1 Corinthians 10:12–13 help us avoid or climb back up the slippery slope of arrogant independence? If you have not already done so, begin memorizing these verses this week.

7. Describe the purpose behind Satan's attempts to separate us from Scripture. How does humble submission to God help us resist his attacks on God's Word?

Applying the Word

1. For a period of one or two days, carry a small notebook (or a tape recorder) and record as many samples of your own speech as possible. Then review those samples prayerfully. Ask the Holy Spirit to search your heart in regard to your speech (Psalm 139:23–24). Does your speech reveal an arrogant, condemning attitude toward others, or a heart given to gentle edification? Cite specific examples to support your conclusion.

Describe your daily routine during a typical week. Be brief but thorough. Then prayerfully consider your typical attitude while pursuing your normal activities. Are you constantly aware of God's sovereign control of your circumstances? Do you frequently think or speak short prayers of gratitude, adoration, confession, and intercession appropriate to various situations? Do particular passages of Scripture come to mind as you react to people and events? Are you acutely aware of God's gracious enablement as you carry out your responsibilities? Evaluate the answers to these questions and determine whether you are behaving as a practical atheist or as a submissive believer.

Meditate on 1 Corinthians 10:12–13 and ask the Lord to make you aware of Satan's specific attempts to drive wedges between you and His Word. Are you tempted to doubt its authority, reliability, or sufficiency? Do you sometimes think that it is irrelevant as a guide for daily living or that you are free to pick and choose among its instructions? Have you sinned by behaving contrary to what you know to be right? If so, cite specific examples.

Complete this application exercise by confessing any and all sin that it has revealed and by praying in accordance Psalm 19:12–14.

2. Choose some creative way to illustrate the idea that *humble submission to God is the key to wise living*. Write a short story or poem, compose a song, perform a skit, or draw a picture or diagram. How could you use your illustration in ministry? Make plans to follow through by putting your illustration to use in some particular way.

Digging Deeper

1. Relate the all-encompassing nature of James's three practical examples in 4:11–17 (see Review Question 2) to the concept of Scripture's reliability and sufficiency.

2. Explain the relationship between God's Law as summarized in the Ten Commandments, Jesus' words in Matthew 22:37–39, and Paul's exhortation to speak "only such a word as is good

"It is God's nature
to make something out of nothing,
that is why He cannot make anything
out of him
who is not yet nothing."

Martin Luther

Chapter Four

A Few Words for the Fools

Come now, you rich, weep and howl for your miseries which are coming upon you. Your riches have rotted and your garments have become moth-eaten. Your gold and your silver have rusted; and their rust will be a witness against you and will consume your flesh like fire. It is in the last days that you have stored up your treasure! Behold, the pay of the laborers who mowed your fields, and which has been withheld by you, cries out against you; and the outcry of those who did the harvesting has reached the ears of the Lord of Sabaoth. You have lived luxuriously on the earth and led a life of wanton pleasure; you have fattened your hearts in a day of slaughter. You have condemned and put to death the righteous man; he does not resist you.
(James 5:1–6)

In the Old Testament book of Proverbs, a wise man named Agur asked two things of God:

Keep deception and lies far from me,
Give me neither poverty nor riches;
Feed me with the food that is my portion,
Lest I be full and deny Thee and say, "Who is the
         Lord?"
Or lest I be in want and steal,
And profane the name of my God. (30:7–9)

The wisdom of Agur is clearly revealed in his requests. He understood the value of truth; and he recognized the depravity of his own heart. By asking the Lord to "keep deception and lies far from [him]," he revealed his commitment to live by "every word that proceeds out of the mouth of God" (Matthew 4:4). And when he asked to be given neither riches nor poverty, he disclosed his sensitivity to his own weakness. He knew that riches would tempt him to arrogant independence, whereas poverty might persuade him to excuse sinful behavior. He also knew that walking down either path would dishonor God and short-circuit his own chief end of being.

Agur's words might remind you of those that James wrote in the early part of his letter: "But let the brother of humble circumstances glory in his high position; and let the rich man glory in his humiliation, because like flowering grass he will pass away. For the sun rises with a scorching wind, and withers the grass; and its flower falls off, and the beauty of its appearance is destroyed; so too the rich man in the midst of his pursuits will fade away" (1:9–11). Although phrased as an exhortation instead of a request, James's words also address the temptations inherent in extreme financial conditions.

James warns the poor man to "glory in his high position"—that is, to remember that straited circumstances do not justify sin. Those who have few earthly possessions must look to the Lord in their need and honor Him with their humble dependence. James then warns the rich man to "glory in his humiliation" by refusing to rely on wealth or position. Those who have been blessed with an abundance of worldly goods must acknowledge God as their source just as He is of salvation.[1]

In these verses James emphasizes the importance of depending on God in the midst of trials, and in 5:1–12 he expands on that theme. Dependence is an essential ingredient of submission to God—which, as we saw in the previous chapter, is the key to wise living.

James underscores this truth boldly in these twelve verses. He first launches a scathing attack on the ungodly rich. These people are not well-meaning believers, temporarily distracted from Christ by their worldly wealth and position. Rather they are those who reject God and His purposes in favor of greed. They spurn the biblical teaching that the world's goods come from God with two conditions attached: they are never to be the source of our hope, and they are to be generously shared with those in need (1 Timothy 6:17–19). In verses 1–6 of Chapter 5, James condemns the foolish rich for their self-indulgence and lack of compassion. He then comforts those whom the rich fools have abused by reminding them of the wisdom of patient endurance (vv. 7-12), which is also involved in submission to God. In this lesson we'll take a look at James's words to the fools; in our next, we'll concentrate on his words to the wise.

The Madness of Materialism

In his tape series *Developing a Christian Mind*, James Mont-gomery Boice makes the profound (and downright startling) point that failure to think Christianly amounts to insanity. What a refreshing perspective that is in a society that charac-terizes radical Christians as ill-equipped for life in the "real world"! Boice condemns society's view as simply ridiculous. The truth is that those who persistently try to think outside of the context of God's absolute sovereignty are, in fact, out of touch with reality![2]

Boice supports his assertion by taking us to the book of Daniel. There we read of Nebuchadnezzar, a powerful king who was driven insane because of his godless thinking. While walking on the roof of his royal palace one day, he reflected and said, "Is this not Babylon the great, which *I myself* have built as a royal residence by the might of my power and for the glory of *my* majesty?" (Daniel 4:29–30, italics added for emphasis).

We would be hard pressed to find a better example of trying to think outside of the context of God's absolute sov-ereignty. And the next few verses describe the price that Nebuchadnezzar paid for such thinking: "[H]e was driven away from mankind and began eating grass like cattle, and his body was drenched with the dew of heaven, until his hair had grown like eagles' feathers and his nails like birds' claws" (vv. 31–33). One of the world's greatest rulers had become completely insane.

God required Nebuchadnezzar to reap what he had sown. Insane behavior invariably results from thinking without a God-centered perspective. The ungodly rich whom James addresses reflect the same truth. They too had divorced God from their patterns of thinking and were thus reaping a life controlled by what John Blanchard calls "the madness of materialism."[3]

These people personified arrogant independence. They had not an ounce of humility in them. Instead of submitting themselves to God's authority and perfect provision, they hoarded the wealth of the world and placed all their trust in it. Their worldly attitude toward money and material goods clearly revealed the state of their hearts. These people were not children of God because they worshipped mammon (Matthew 6:24).

James speaks to them in terms of condemnation, not only to warn them of impending judgment but also to encourage the hearts of those they were abusing. "[W]eep and howl," he commands them, "for your miseries which are coming upon you. Your riches have rotted and your garments have become moth-eaten. Your gold and your silver have rusted; and their rust will be a witness against you and will consume your flesh like fire. It is in the last days that you have stored up your treasure!" (5: 1–3).

These ungodly rich were tragically out of touch with reality. Because they had refused to acknowledge God as the source of all good things (James 1:17), they would eventually see those good things disintegrate. Because they selfishly had spurned God's purpose for wealth (1 John 3:17–18), they would soon hear their tarnished riches bear witness against them. Stored-up worldly treasure would do them no good when they stood before the Judge of the Universe to give an account of their lives (Matthew 6:19–21). They had made the deadly mistake of allowing their riches to possess them instead of possessing their riches to the glory of God.

John Blanchard says that the only cure for the madness of materialism is the sanity of stewardship.[4] The ungodly rich are doomed to destruction unless they return to their senses—as did Nebuchadnezzar. In the book of Daniel, he tells us what happened: "But at the end of that period [of insanity] I, Nebuchadnezzar, raised my eyes toward heaven, and my reason returned to me, and I blessed the Most High and praised and honored Him who lives forever;

> *For His dominion is an everlasting dominion,*
> *And His kingdom endures from generation to*
> *generation.*
> *And all the inhabitants of the earth are accounted as*
> *nothing.*
> *But He does according to His will in the host of heaven*
> *And among the inhabitants of earth;*
> *And no one can ward off His hand*
> *Or say to Him, 'What hast Thou done?'*

"At that time my reason returned to me. And . . . I was reestablished in my sovereignty, and surpassing greatness was added to me. Now I Nebuchadnezzar praise, exalt, and honor the King of heaven, for all His works are true and His ways just, and He is able to humble those who walk in pride" (4:34–37).

Nebuchadnezzar was, at long last, equipped for life in the real world—the world as it actually is—governed by God. Unfortunately, James gives us no indication that the ungodly rich to whom he was speaking ever learned that wise lesson.

Greed Breeds Indulgence and Strangles Compassion

Contrary to what some people believe, there is nothing intrinsically evil in wealth, nor is there any inherent value in poverty. Many of God's most faithful saints have been rich, and just as many (or more) of the world's greatest sinners have been poverty-stricken.

Both conditions of life carry their own peculiar blessings and curses. The rich have the resources (and usually the ability and influence) to accomplish a great deal in ministry, whereas the poor often excel in the virtues of humility, submission, kindness, patience, and (interestingly) generosity. However, the rich also are quite prone to an inordinate delight in the things of this world, to arrogant independence from God, and to self-indulgent stinginess. The poor, on the other hand, constantly battle temptation in the form of inordinate desires for the things of this world, accusatory thoughts about God, and consuming self-pity.

In verse 4 of Chapter 5, James confronts the unrighteous rich with a sin representative of their godless attitude. "Behold, the pay of the laborers who mowed your fields, and which has been withheld by you, cries out against you; and the outcry of those who did the harvesting has reached the ears of the Lord of Sabaoth." The rich had been carried away and enticed by their lust for the things of the world; that lust had conceived an attitude of self-indulgent greed, which in turn had given birth to the act of defying God's laws. That attitude and behavior, if not confessed and forgiven, would lead to death. (See James 1:14–15.)

God had decreed in His Word that employers must deal with their employees *compassionately*. They were not to "oppress a hired servant . . . [but to] give him his wages on his day before the sun sets, for he is poor and sets his heart on it; so that he may not cry against you to the Lord and it become sin in you" (Deuteronomy 24:14–15). The prophet Jeremiah had warned against allowing self-indulgent greed to strangle compassion:

> *Woe to him who builds his house without righteousness*
> *And his upper rooms without justice,*
> *Who uses his neighbor's services without pay*
> *And does not give him his wages (22:13).*

And Malachi had made clear how God would respond when abused laborers cried out to Him in their distress: "'Then I will draw near to you for judgment; and I will be a swift witness against . . . those who oppress the wage earner in his wages . . . and do not fear Me,' says the Lord of hosts" (3:5).

Power, position, and wealth are always "on loan" from God. Wise stewards see them as a means of dispensing our Father's compassion to his needy children; however, fools like the ones James is addressing give in to their selfish passions and set themselves up for the judgment of God.

Greed Never Wins

Self-indulgent greed is tragically foolish because it never wins. Perhaps in this case, the rather irreverent statement "God will get you for that" is entirely appropriate! The great Bible commentator Matthew Henry has explained: "The Lord of hosts, who has all ranks of beings and creatures at his disposal, and who sets all in their several places, hears the oppressed when they cry by reason of cruelty or injustice of the oppressor, and he will give orders to some of those hosts that are under him . . . to avenge the wrongs done to those who are dealt with unrighteously and unmercifully."[5]

Lord of Sabaoth is the name of God used in the Bible to describe His majestic power as ruler of the world and commander of the hosts of heaven.[6] James uses it here with good reason: He wants to underscore God's sovereign authority to judge the unrighteous, as well as His merciful goodness in defending the downtrodden. God, the all-powerful ruler, will surely condemn the greedy rich who have uselessly hoarded and self-indulgently have spent their unjustly gained and ruthlessly acquired wealth.

God is the dispenser of all material goods. He bestows them for the purpose of exalting His glory. Those who foolishly disdain their stewardship privileges will pay a high price. And this truth applies to believers and unbelievers alike. Keep in mind that even though James is speaking about unbelievers in this part of his letter, he is also speaking to Christians. Therefore, his words have a definite double edge to them. They are both an encouraging reminder to the oppressed of God's certain judgment and a convicting warning to wealthy Christians against committing this sin.

James is not the only writer of Scripture who dwells on these issues. The Psalms are replete with encouragement for the abused, with Psalms 37 and 73 being two good examples. And the New Testament echoes with exhortations regarding the proper way to use wealth. Matthew and Luke record Jesus' teaching that no one can serve more than one master (Matthew 6:24; Luke 16:9–13). In Acts we see the early Church's sterling example of sharing to meet needs (4:32–35). Paul exhorted his protégé, Timothy, to "[i]nstruct those who are rich in this present world not to be conceited or to fix their hope on the uncertainty of riches, but on God, who richly supplies us with all things to enjoy. Instruct them to do good, to be rich in good works, to be generous and ready to share, storing up for themselves the treasure of a good foundation for the future, so that they may take hold of that which is life indeed" (1 Timothy 6:17–19). And John cautioned those who had "the world's goods" not to close their hearts against a "brother in need" (1 John 3:17–18).

There should be no doubt in our minds that those who, in James's words, have "lived luxuriously on the earth and led a life of wanton pleasure; . . . have fattened [their] hearts in a day of slaughter. . . . [and] condemned and put to death the righteous man" (5:5–6) are flagrantly violating God's commandments in Scripture. The righteous, however, should not lose heart and become discouraged. The Lord of Sabaoth is their powerful sovereign, who always deals justly. In our next chapter, we'll see how they can live wisely in a "real world" full of distress by patiently trusting in Him.

[1] These verses were covered in depth in chapter 4 of James on Trials.

[2] James Montgomery Boice, *Developing a Christian Mind: Preparing People to Think and Act Biblically* (Philadelphia: The Bible Study Hour, nd), tape 2 of 4.

[3] John Blanchard, *Truth For Life: A Devotional Commentary on the Epistle of James* (Durham, England: Evangelical Press, 1986), 338.

[4] *Ibid.*

[5] Matthew Henry, *Matthew Henry's Commentary on the Whole Bible: Volume 6, Acts to Revelation* (Peabody, Mass.: Hendrickson Publishers, 1991), 801.

[6] D. Edmond Hiebert, *James* (Chicago: Moody Press, 1979, 1992), 266.

Review Questions

1. How does Agur's prayer in Proverbs 30:8–9 relate to James's exhortation in 1:9–11 of his letter to those living in extreme financial conditions? Read James 5:1–12 in the light of Proverbs 30:8–9 and James 1:9–11; then explain how the rich and the poor each have special needs for God's wisdom.

2. Using the example of Nebuchadnezzar in Daniel 4:28–37, explain in your own words why trying to think outside of the context of God's absolute sovereignty amounts to insanity.

3. Describe "the madness of materialism." What is its only cure, according to John Blanchard? How does Nebuchadnezzar's example support John Blanchard's assertion?

4. List some of the peculiar blessings and curses of both wealth and poverty. Do you think walking worthy of their high calling in Christ is more difficult for the rich or for the poor? Explain your answer.

5. Summarize the requirements that God places on employers. Use the verses you studied in this chapter and any others of which you may be aware. Then relate the behavior of the employers whom James addresses in 5:4 to his earlier teaching in 1:14–15. What attitudes are revealed in their behavior?

6. What attributes of God are captured in the name *Lord of Sabaoth?* Why did James choose to use this name of God in his words to the ungodly rich?

7. Describe the encouragement and the warning to believers contained in James 5:1–6.

Applying the Word

1. Read Psalms 37 and 73 carefully, filling in the following
    chart:

God's specific instructions to believers	Ways in which God cares for His children	Ways in which God will deal with the wicked

Are you being subjected to mistreatment, injustice, or oppression in your life right now? If so, briefly describe your situation. If not, do you know someone who is? If so, describe his or her situation.

How has your study of Psalms 37 and 73 deepened your understanding of God as the Lord of Sabaoth?

How will this deepened understanding of God help you think about your situation (or the situation of the person you know) within the context of God's absolute sovereignty?

How will this kind of thinking change your attitude toward your situation? Explain. How does it better equip you to help others who are in distress? Explain.

Digging Deeper

1. According to Martin Luther, "It is God's nature to make something out of nothing, that is why He cannot make anything out of him who is not yet nothing." Relate his statement to what you have learned in Chapters Three and Four about the wisdom of submitting to God and the foolishness of arrogant independence.

"A man with God on his side
is always in the majority."

John Knox

Chapter Five

Genuine Wisdom Hopes Patiently

Be patient, therefore, brethren, until the coming of the Lord. Behold, the farmer waits for the precious produce of the soil, being patient about it, until it gets the early and late rains. You too be patient; strengthen your hearts, for the coming of the Lord is at hand. Do not complain, brethren, against one another, that you yourselves may not be judged; behold, the Judge is standing right at the door. As an example, brethren, of suffering and patience, take the prophets who spoke in the name of the Lord. Behold, we count those blessed who endured. You have heard of the endurance of Job and have seen the outcome of the Lord's dealings, that the Lord is full of compassion and is merciful. But above all, my brethren, do not swear, either by heaven or by earth or with any other oath; but let your yes be yes, and your no, no; so that you may not fall under judgment. (James 5:7–12)

I'm sure you've heard evangelistic appeals that sound something like this: "What have you got to lose by becoming a Christian? If you receive Christ and there is an afterlife, you will spend it in heaven—but even if there isn't, your life here on earth will be much better with Him than without Him." Sounds like a logical, persuasive approach, right? I always thought so until someone suggested I reread 1Corinthians 15 to get Paul's perspective. And since Paul's perspective is certainly more important than mine, let me suggest that you do the same before you read on.

Did you discover, as I did, that "the world's greatest evangelist" didn't use the approach that sounds so persuasive and logical? First Corinthians 15:12–19, in particular. makes that fact very clear:

> *Now if Christ is preached, that He has been raised from the dead, how do some among you say that there is no resurrection of the dead? But if there is no resurrection of the dead, not even Christ has been raised; and if Christ has not been raised, **then our preaching is vain, your faith also is vain**. Moreover we are even found to be **false witnesses of God,** because we witnessed against God that He raised Christ, whom He did not raise, if in fact the dead are not raised. For if the dead are not raised, not even Christ has been raised; and if Christ has not been raised, **your faith is worthless; you are still in your sins**. Then those also who have fallen asleep in Christ have perished. If we have hoped in Christ **in this life only**, we are of all men most to be pitied"* (**bold** type added for emphasis).

Paul knew that preaching "What have you got to lose?" is vain and produces a *vain faith* for at least three reasons. First of all, such an approach misrepresents absolute truth by allowing the possibility that it might not be true. Paul persistently and consistently affirmed the undeniable fact of Christ's resurrection because to do anything else would make him *a false witness* of God (v. 15).

Secondly, this kind of preaching appeals to the short-sighted concerns of fallen humanity instead of to our real need—which is eternal. Even if having faith in an unresurrected Redeemer could help us live in happiness and contentment (and I'm not sure it could), it does not change the reality of an afterlife in which we will be judged. Christ's resurrection marks God's acceptance of full payment for the sins of His children. If it did not occur, then our faith is worthless because we are still in our sins (v. 17). And if we are still in our sins, we will be judged unfit to live in eternity with the God whose eyes are too pure to look upon evil and condone wrongdoing (Habakkuk 1:13).

Finally, Paul indicates that such preaching distorts the message of the Gospel by fixing our hope in this world instead of the next. Paul knew that this world is full of suffering, and that Christ had promised His followers more of the same (Matthew 5:10–12). Therefore, if we hope in Christ *in this life only*, we are of all people most to be pitied (1 Corinthians 15:19).

Of course, the great bedrock Gospel truth of Christ's resurrection supports our approach to wise Christian living just as well as it does our approach to evangelism. Our teacher, James, echoes Paul's thinking as he reminds suffering believers that their hope in Christ is anchored *not in this life only*, but in eternity. That is what gives them the patience to "suffer long" with those who abuse them.

Wise Hope Builds Patient Faith

Genuine wisdom is rooted, grounded, and shot through with hope because it *enjoys* submitting to God's comforting sovereignty. Truly wise people are happy because they are humble. They know they were created dependent on God for every aspect of life, and their greatest satisfaction results from obedient trust. The scriptural truths they are learning about God and His work anchor their hope in His promises of future perfection rather than in this world's shaky foundations. The more secure their hope grows, the more patient their faith; and the more patient their faith, the greater their joy.

John Blanchard, in his book *Truth for Life*, alludes to this anchor of hope when he says, "Biblical patience is not rooted in fatalism that says everything is out of control. It is rooted in faith that says everything is in God's control."[1] As God's Holy Spirit deepens our understanding of His oversight of the distress in the world to accomplish His purposes, we learn to *hope joyfully* by looking beyond the things that are seen to the things that aren't seen (Isaiah 40:7–8; Jeremiah 29:11–13; 2 Corinthians 4:16–18).

Such God-centered hope equips us to obey our Father's command to "Rest in the Lord and wait patiently for Him" (Psalm 37:7)—in other words, to exercise wise, patient faith. Wise Christians know that God loves them too much to allow them to suffer without a good reason (Jeremiah 29:11; 31:3; Romans 8:32). They know that He will never leave them to suffer alone and unaided (Matthew 28:20; 1Corinthians 10:13; Hebrews 13:5–6). And they know that all righteous suffering is temporary and generates a reward that is well worth the effort (Romans 8:18; 1 Peter 5:10).

Wise Christians have counted the cost of their discipleship and expect to suffer as a result of their obedience to the call of Christ. They welcome the assurance that builds as persecution and hardship test their allegiance to His perfection and power while it underscores His magnificent worth as full compensation and prize (Philippians 3:12–14). They understand Satan's desire to twist into something evil the suffering that God intended for good (Genesis 50:20); and they resist his attempts to pervert God's necessary good work of purifying our faith. Wise Christians agree with Paul's teaching that Christianity was never meant to be a good way to "maximize pleasure" in this present life (1 Corinthians 15:32). And they pronounce a hearty "Amen!" to James's assertion of our need for patience because we will not know maximum pleasure until the Lord Jesus returns.[2]

"Be patient, therefore, brethren," James now advises his readers, "until the coming of the Lord. Behold, the farmer waits for the precious produce of the soil, being patient about it, until it gets the early and late rains. You too be patient; strengthen your hearts, for the coming of the Lord is at hand" (5:7–8). The Greek word James uses here to refer to the Lord's second coming is *parousia*—a word that speaks of authority and power and is frequently used to describe the arrival of an emperor or king.[3] Knowledgeable Christians know that Christ first came in humility for the purpose of living and dying in subordination to God to secure our salvation.

They know that His resurrection and ascension marked His exaltation to the right hand of God(Acts 2:33), where today He exercises "[a]ll authority . . . in heaven and on earth" (Matthew 28:18). And they know that He will come again in power to end the curse (Romans 8:20–21), overthrow evil (Revelation 20:10–15), and usher in God's eternal Kingdom (21:1–8).

Wise Christians, however, move beyond knowledge to application. They use what they know as the basis for hope that equips them to be patient in trying circumstances. Their patience does not take the form of fatalistic complacency, stoical insensitivity, nor irrational denials of evil's reality. Rather, it rejoices to submit every aspect of life to the God who is sovereign. Wise Christians display patient faith because they act upon God's revealed truth. They cast all their anxiety upon Him because they know He cares for them (1 Peter 5:7) and that He will perfect the good work He has begun in them (Philippians 1:6).

Just like a wise farmer who patiently accepts hardship and distress for the sake of a good crop, wise Christians "consider it all joy" when they patiently "suffer long" for the sake of God's promises. May we exercise that kind of wisdom!

How Patience Behaves

The certainty of our faith in Christ's second coming not only equips us to wait patiently for it; it also shapes our behavior while we are waiting. George Bernard Shaw captured this characteristic of faith when he said, "Our conduct is influenced not so much by our experience as by our expectations."[4]

Wise patient faith is slow to anger (James 1:19–20) and doesn't complain (5:9) because it rests in the hopeful assurance of full vindication at Christ's Second Coming. Christians who exercise such faith do so with the understanding that God is the righteous Judge of the wicked as well as their loving Father. They can endure all things now because they have learned from the sterling examples of patient saints of the past that "the outcome of the Lord's dealings" reveals His compassion and mercy toward His chosen children (vv. 10–11).

Their attitude and behavior should not be construed as a validation of evil, nor as passive resistance to fate, but as purposeful self–restraint that draws on the power of God's Holy Spirit to resist hasty retaliation when they face provocation. Those who exercise wise, patient faith would agree with D. Edmond Hiebert when he asserts, "Christianity is strongly opposed to all forms of social injustice, but it also urges believers to maintain a proper attitude and perspective amid such injustices."[5] Wise, patient Christians submit to God's sovereign working of *all things*—even injustice and evil—together for good to accomplish His purposes (Genesis 50:20; Acts 2:23–24; Romans 8:28).

Having highlighted this truth in vv. 7–8, James cautions his readers against complaining (v. 9) and swearing (v. 12). He knew that impatience in tribulation leads to anger expressed in irritation, slander, and wrath against those who practice oppression. Such actions generate an atmosphere of discontentment and self-assertion, which fosters complaint against Christian brothers and sisters as well as self-reliant oath-taking. This kind of behavior interferes with the pursuit of the believers' chief end by robbing them of their joy and thus dishonoring God.

When we as Christians allow persecution and trouble to affect us this way, James says we can expect to be judged (v. 9). Of course, this "judgment" differs from what the wicked will bear, in that it is disciplinary and does not condemn us (Jeremiah 2:18–19; Romans 8:1; Hebrews 12:5–8; 1 Peter 4:17). James seems to be cautioning us to remember that even though discipline has value for our sanctification, it should be avoided if possible. Not only is it decidedly unpleasant, but it also sidelines us for a time from useful service to God.

When we exercise wise, patient faith by enduring all things in the hope of Christ's coming, we can rejoice with Asaph the psalmist, who proclaimed in the midst of difficulty and trial:

> *Whom have I in heaven but Thee?*
> *And besides Thee, I desire nothing on earth.*
> *My flesh and my heart may fail,*
> *But God is the strength of my heart and my portion forever.*
> *For, behold, those who are far from Thee will perish;*
> *Thou hast destroyed all those who are unfaithful to Thee.*
> *But as for me, the nearness of God is my good;*
> *I have made the Lord God my refuge,*
> *That I may tell of all Thy works. (Psalm 73:25–28)*

1   John Blanchard, T*ruth For Life: A Devotional Commentary on the Epistle of James* (Durham, England: Evangelical Press, 1986), 348.

2   Much of the information in this paragraph comes from Chapter 10 of John Piper's *Desiring God: Meditations of a Christian Hedonist* (Sisters Ore.: Multnomah Books, 1986, 1996). This chapter was added to the 1996 edition of Piper's thought-stirring book and contains many refreshing insights into the nature and purpose of suffering. If you haven't read it, I urge you to do so.

3   Blanchard, *Truth for Life*, 341.

4   Quoted in *ibid*, 343.

5   D. Edmond Hiebert, *James* (Chicago: Moody Press, 1979, 1992), 259. Original title, *The Epistle of James*.

Review Questions

1. Reread 1 Corinthians 15 carefully and then use what you've read to respond to this question: "Would Paul have used (or approved of) the 'What have you got to lose?' method of evangelism?"

2. Describe the relationship between our hope in Christ and patient faith.

3. Explain how genuine wisdom generates joy. Support your reasoning with Scripture.

4. Write a brief character sketch of a Christian who has learned to exercise wise, patient faith.

5. James reminds his readers of the Lord's second coming as an incentive for them to exercise patience. Explain how this reminder motivates believers to be patient in difficulty.

6. Explain how George Bernard Shaw's words, "Our conduct is influenced not so much by our experience as by our expectations," summarize what James teaches in 5:9–12.

7. If you have not done so already, memorize Psalm 73:25–28

Applying the Word

1. List five or more things (possibly including people) in which worldly minded people seek security. Then ask the Lord's help in prayer to examine your heart and discover how much you depend on these things for your security in this life. Describe the one(s) upon which you are most tempted to depend.

Read and meditate on Isaiah 40:3–31, Jeremiah 29:11–13; 2 Corinthians 4:7–18, and Philippians 3:1–14. In the spaces below summarize the teaching of each of these passages regarding the only legitimate source of your secure hope as a believer.

Isaiah 40:3–31:

Jeremiah 29:11–13:

2 Corinthians 4:7–18:

Philippians 3:1–14:

Now describe specific thoughts, attitudes, and behavior that you should change in order to begin seeking your security in the right places. Devise a step-by-step plan that will help you make one or more of these changes; then share your plan with someone who loves you enough to hold you accountable.

2. Describe three or more specific examples *from your own life* of how a secure hope in Christ's Second Coming will help you develop wise, patient faith. How will developing wise, patient faith equip you to minister to others in your family or your circle of friends? In answering this question, think about to whom you will minister, *when* and *where* you will minister to them, what you will do for them, and how (with what kind of attitude) you will minister to them.

3. For a period of one week, pay particular attention to your own speech with the intent of evaluating how much you complain. Listen carefully to the ways you respond verbally to people and events in your daily routine. Do your words reflect confident trust in God's sovereign control of every circumstance of life? Is your example as encouraging to other believers as that of the prophets and Job? What specific changes should you make in your speech in order to reflect more accurately the great power of God and to be a better example to others? How will you implement those needed changes?

Digging Deeper

1. Two Greek words are frequently translated into English
   as patience. One is *makrothumeō*; the other is hupomonē. Using
   an exhaustive concordance, Bible dictionary, Greek lexicon,
   and/or other appropriate reference books, look up these two
   words and determine the differences in meaning between
   them. Then use an interlinear Bible (or the Greek text, if you
   know the language) and determine which of these two words
   James used in 1:2–3 and 5:7–8 of his letter. Given the context of
   these passages, explain James's choice of words (*makrothumeō*
   vs. *hupomonē*) in each of these instances. Be sure to include in
   your explanation what his pastoral as well as linguistic reasons
   might have been for using the words that he did.

"It is good having those for friends whose prayers are available in the sight of God."

Matthew Henry

Chapter Six

Genuine Wisdom Prays

Is anyone among you suffering? Let him pray. Is anyone cheerful? Let him sing praises. Is anyone among you sick? Let him call for the elders of the church, and let them pray over him, anointing him with oil in the name of the Lord; and the prayer offered in faith will restore the one who is sick, and the Lord will raise him up, and if he has committed sins, they will be forgiven him. Therefore, confess your sins to one another, and pray for one another, so that you may be healed. The effective prayer of a righteous man can accomplish much. Elijah was a man with a nature like ours, and he prayed earnestly that it might not rain; and it did not rain on the earth for three years and six months. And he prayed again, and the sky poured rain, and the earth produced its fruit. (James 5:13–18)

"Prayer is the antidote for the disease of self–confidence."[1]

That sentence is vintage John Piper. It packs the essence of why genuine wisdom prays into one concise sentence—and, in the process, packs quite a wallop. Piper has a rare gift for conveying a vast wealth of meaning in a paucity of words, as this sentence well illustrates. Indeed, everything that I'll be saying in this chapter, he concisely expresses here in ten simple words! But even so, I must urge you to resist the temptation of skipping straight to the questions. You see, one of the greatest delights in reading John Piper is pausing to "unpack" one of his loaded sentences.

I encountered this one while preparing to work through his book *Desiring God: Meditations of a Christian Hedonist* with my friend Angela. At the time, I was also researching this book on James. Perhaps that is why I was struck by the way Piper's sentence so aptly summarizes James's teaching on the wisdom of prayer.

Now if you're thinking, *I've just read James 5:13–18 and Piper's sentence, but I don't see the connection,* don't feel too bad. It helps to have read the ten pages he wrote about prayer that lead up to that sentence! In those pages he reminds us of several significant and helpful biblical truths. First and foremost, he reasserts God's intense interest in displaying the fullness of His own glory by "spilling over" that fullness in mercy to us.[2] The end result of that intense interest Piper expresses like this: "When we humble ourselves like little children and put on no airs of self-sufficiency, but run happily into the joy of our Father's embrace, the glory of His grace is magnified and the longing of our soul is satisfied."[3]

Piper then takes us to the Upper Room Discourse (John 13–16), where he revisits the facts that prayer is a means of pursuing God's glory (14:13), that it is also a means of pursuing our joy (16:24), and that it enables us to pursue both of those things by asking God to do for us through Christ what we can't do for ourselves (15:7). Piper elaborates on these great truths: "Prayer is the open admission that without Christ we can do nothing. And prayer is the turning away from ourselves to God in confidence that he will provide the help we need. Prayer humbles us as needy, and exalts God as wealthy."[4]

Piper also emphasizes that those who know Jesus best will ask the most from Him (because they best understand their own need and God's full provision [John 4:9–10]) and that when we "call upon [Him] in the day of trouble" we will be delivered, but He must get the glory (Psalm 50:15).[5]

Having said all that, Piper takes us to James 4:3–5. This passage, he says, pictures a kind of prayer that God will condemn. The Church is here portrayed as an unfaithful wife who seeks from the world the pleasures she should seek from her Husband (God) and then has the audacity to ask her Husband for the resources she needs to pursue her unfaithfulness. Piper's summary of James 4:3–5 is downright shocking: "We use our Husband's generosity to hire prostitutes for private pleasures."[6] But perhaps we need to be shocked. We all find it easier to pray "with wrong motives, so that [we] may spend it on our pleasures" (v. 3) than we do to pray with our hearts intent upon exalting God and delighting in Him.

Therefore, wise prayer *makes the effort* to acknowledge our own helplessness and His perfect power, to call upon Him for the help that we desperately need to be righteous, and earnestly to seek His counsel concerning the affairs of our daily lives. It is at this point that Piper says, "Prayer is the antidote for the disease of self-confidence."

Are you beginning to see the connection between the teaching contained in James 5:13–18 and Piper's rich sentence? Genuine wisdom prays because it recognizes its utter dependence upon the Creator for every aspect of life. Prayer is thus an act of submission, which, we already have seen, is the key to wise living.

"Prayer" Is the Right Answer to Every Question

If you grew up going to Sunday School, you may identify with the young boy who insightfully assured one nervous visitor, "Don't worry. No matter what question the teacher asks, the right answer is 'Jesus.'" But if you've thought through the verses that begin this chapter, you may be tempted to add, "Unless the teacher is James—then the right answer is 'prayer.'"

James asks his distressed readers three pertinent questions; then he answers each one with the same essential response.

Q: Is anyone among you suffering?
A: Let him pray.
Q: Is anyone cheerful?
A: Let him sing praises.[7]
Q: Is anyone among you sick?

A: Let him call for the elders of the church,
and let them pray over him, anointing him
with oil in the name of the Lord.

The first question is obviously rhetorical. James knew they were suffering. His awareness of and concern for their suffering prompted his letter. He already has spilled a great deal of ink reminding them of their all-sufficient resources in Christ, resources that will comfort and sustain them through the difficulties of life. He has described the nature of genuine faith and extolled the virtues of "the wisdom from above" as the means of living out their high calling in Christ. Now with characteristic practicality, he exhorts them to pray—not only in troubled times, but in all situations of life. Yes, of course, pray when you're suffering, he tells them. But also pray when you're happy, and when you're weak.

With these three questions, James emphasizes what our basic attitude should be toward life's mutability. No matter what comes our way, our response should be prayer. The Puritan Thomas Manton captured the key thought of James's teaching in this exquisite sentence: "It is the perfection of Christianity to have a constant mind in changing states."[8] Then he went on to affirm that the best way of acquiring and maintaining that constant mind is through consistent communion with the One who directs and controls those changing states.

Alec Motyer has expressed the same concept a bit more effusively: "Our whole life . . . should be so angled towards God that whatever strikes upon us, whether sorrow or joy, should be deflected upwards at once into His presence."[9] And David, on the day that the Lord delivered him from his enemies, voiced it poetically in Psalm 18:

"I love Thee, O LORD, *my strength."*
The LORD *is my rock and my fortress and my*
          deliverer,
My God, my rock, in whom I take refuge;
My shield and the horn of my salvation, my
          stronghold. . . .
As for God, His way is blameless. . . .
For who is God, but the LORD?
And who is a rock, except our God,
The God who girds me with strength,
And makes my way blameless? . . .
Thou hast also given me the shield of Thy
          salvation,
And Thy right hand upholds me. . . .
The LORD *lives, and blessed be my rock;*
And exalted be the God of my salvation. . . .
Therefore I will give thanks to Thee among the
          nations, O LORD,
And I will sing praises to Thy name
(vv. 1–2, 30, 31–32, 35, 46, 49).

Faith at work turns every situation of life over to God
in prayer, seeking the pure wisdom that infuses every situation with meaning and purpose. When we pray at all times
with the help of His Spirit (Ephesians 6:18), we see our difficulties, delights, and weaknesses from His perspective instead of our own. And we trade the deadly disease of self-
confidence for the glowing health of trusting fully in God
(Psalm 40:4; Jeremiah 17:5–8).

Some Controversial Verses

If you've been involved in Bible study for very long, you are no doubt aware that James 5:14–15 has generated great controversy within the Body of Christ. Protestants have long disagreed with Roman Catholics, who base their sacrament of extreme unction upon this passage. Some Christians claim these verses as a guaranteed formula for miraculous physical healing, whereas others assert that James is not speaking of physical healing at all but is wholly concerned with our spiritual health. Others Christians admit they don't know who's right and who's wrong, but they take the "elder and oil" route when they are sick simply because the Bible commands it.

Well, if you are looking to me for the definitive answer, you're going to be disappointed. Since I am neither a trained theologian nor a church officer, I am not qualified to speak definitively on this thorny passage of Scripture. However, as a weak but Spirit-led lay person (just like most of you), I can and will give you two helpful guidelines for understanding these verses.

First and foremost, consider the passage within both its immediate and broader contexts. James is discussing the wisdom of prayer; therefore, the words in these verses must be consistent with what he (and the rest of the Bible) teaches about both wisdom and prayer. If you take the time to investigate the whole counsel of God on these two topics, you will discover that "wise prayer" looks exactly the way that James describes it: It is offered to God *in the name of the Lord*, and it is offered *in faith*. (See John 14:13–14, 15:16, 16:23–24; James 1:6–8; 1 John 3:21–22, 5:13–15.) In other words, such prayer is offered in accord with His mind, on His authority, and within His will.[10]

You will also discover that wise prayer is *effective* because its primary concern is the glory of God and the accomplishment of His purposes. John Blanchard describes it as "circular in shape; it begins and ends in heaven, in the sovereign will of God."[11] And D. Edmond Hiebert suggests that James's unconditional language in this passage is explained by the fact that wise prayer reflects God's will in the matter instead of the will of a person.[12] Therefore, prayers for healing will be effective when they reflect God's mind on the matter rather than ours.

The second guideline is to make use of some good reference books (or reliable commentaries) to learn all you can about the word sick, the function of elders in the Church, and about the use of oil in the Middle East during the first century. Since so much of the controversy surrounding this passage hovers around those three things, you need to know that sick is the Greek word *asthenei*, which means "without strength"; that elders have been particularly called and gifted to speak to God on behalf of their flock; and that oil was used medicinally at that time and place. Those facts won't give you all the answers you want, but they will help you think clearly about what James is saying.

It seems to me that his words about healing urge believers to pray wisely in any and all weakness—be it physical, mental, moral, or spiritual—with two thoughts in mind:

(1) A weakness in any one of these areas will eventually affect all the others, and (2) our weaknesses are intended to show forth God's glory by demonstrating His power, either in healing the weakness or in enabling us to serve Him effectively in weakness. Wise prayer seeks out and requests His will for each situation.

The Effective Prayers of the Righteous

When we pray wisely, James assures us that God will answer. "[A]nd the prayer offered in faith (and in the name of the Lord; see v. 14) will restore the one who is sick, and the Lord will raise him up, and if he has committed sins, they will be forgiven him" (5:15).

Although that statement may sound astounding when pulled out of context, it is no more amazing than these words of John: "And this is the confidence which we have before Him, that, if we ask anything according to His will, He hears us. And if we know that He hears us in whatever we ask, we know that we have requests which we have asked from Him" (1 John 5:14–15). Answered prayer should not come as a surprise to us, for we are God's children. Indeed, such a surprise may indicate that we are not in the habit of praying wisely.

Since God answers wise prayers, James tells us to "confess your sins to one another, and pray for one another, so that you may be healed. The effective prayer of a righteous man can accomplish much" (v. 16). The repeated reference to sin in verses 15–16 has led many competent commentators to the conclusion that James is limiting his assurances to spiritual healing—and they may be right. However, his concluding sentence in verse 16 has given me a slightly different perspective. Could he be saying that righteous people pray wisely (and thus effectively) because righteousness requires confession of sin—and that confession of sin enhances our ability to seek out and submit to God's will for a particular circumstance—and that when we pray for God's will in that circumstance, He will answer our prayers? For what it's worth, I give you that suggestion. Please act like a Berean (see Acts 17:11) and also consider the opinions of others more learned than I am before you accept it.

James caps his remarks about prayer with a stunning example of what the righteous can do when they wisely submit to God's purposes and then pray accordingly. If you have not read 1 Kings 17–18 recently, please take a moment to do so before going on. James's references to Elijah's rain prayers spotlight this portion of the Old Testament; therefore, I am assuming that he intends the whole passage to illustrate and support his teaching on prayer.

Did you notice the wide variety of miracles God performed in response to the prayers of His servant, Elijah, at that time in history? God not only controlled the weather, created food, and raised a child from the dead (physical miracles), but He also changed a woman's mind (a mental miracle) and soundly defeated the prophets of Baal in a test of strength (a spiritual miracle). Did you also notice that all of these miraculous answers to prayer came because Elijah prayed wisely in faith, being assured of God's will for the situation? Surely that is why James refers us to him as a prayer warrior worthy of our emulation.

1   John Piper, *Desiring God: Mediations of a Christian Hedonist*, (Sisters, Ore.: Multinomah Books, 1986, 1996), 146.

2   See Psalm 37 for an excellent biblical example of how the fullness of God's glory spills over in mercy to His children.

3   Piper, *Desiring God*, 137.

4   Ibid, 138.

5   Ibid, 139–140.

6   Ibid, 141.

7   Although James doesn't use the word *pray* in this response, we can infer it safely. The Bible consistently teaches that praise and worship of God is the central element of righteous prayer. For a fuller discussion of this subject, see Lesson 5 of my book *Before the Throne of God: Focus on Prayer,* Light for Your Path Series (Phillipsburg, NJ: P & R Publishing, 1999).

8   Thomas Manton, *The Crossway Classic Commentaries: James,* series editors Alister McGrath and J. I. Packer (Wheaton, Ill.: Crossway Books, 1995), 328.

9   Quoted in John Blanchard, *Truth For Life: A Devotional Commentary on the Epistle of James* (Durham, England: Evangelical Press, 1986), 363.

10 See my Light for Your Path study *Before the Throne of God: Focus on Prayer* (referenced at [7] above) for a fuller discussion of these issues.

11 Blanchard, *Truth for Life,* 377.

12 D. Edmond Hiebert, *James* (Chicago: Moody Press, 1979, 1992), 297. Original title, *The Epistle of James*.

Review Questions

1. John Piper said, "Prayer is the antidote for the disease of self-confidence." In your own words, briefly explain how his words capture concisely the wisdom of prayer. Feel free to draw on what you have learned in previous chapters as well as in this one.

2. List the three occasions to which James says we should respond with prayer. (If you haven't read footnote [7], do so now.) Why do you think James chose these three situations to emphasize the wisdom of prayer?

3. What do the quotations from Thomas Manton, Alec Motyer, and David on page 127 tell us about the wisdom of prayer?

4. Explain how the two guidelines listed below help us understand James's teaching in the controversial verses, 5:14–15:

The guideline of context:

The guideline of key words and concepts:

5. What does wise prayer "look like" and what makes it effective? Read John 14:13–14, 15:16, 16:23–24; James 1:6–8; 1 John 3:21–22, 5:13–15 before attempting to answer this question and support your answer using those verses.

6. Describe the relationship between forgiveness of sin and wise prayer. Can an unrighteous person pray wisely? Why or why not?

7. Drawing on what you read in 1 Kings 17–18, explain why Elijah is a prayer warrior worthy of our emulation.

Applying the Word

1. Using the following chart, list what you consider to be your
    primary strengths and weaknesses physically, mentally, mor-
    ally, and spiritually. (HINT: A weakness is not a sin; see 2
    Corinthians 12:7–10.) Before you begin, ask God to help you
    examine yourself (Psalm 139:23–24; Jeremiah 17:9–10). Be spe-
    cific and current in your evaluation.

	Strengths	Weaknesses
Physical		
Mental		
Moral		
Spiritual		

Consider your completed chart carefully; then answer the following questions.

Do you see evidence of a strength or weakness in one area affecting other areas? If so, explain.

How might each strength and weakness tempt you to sin?

How might each strength and weakness glorify God?

What was God's purpose in creating you with this particular set of strengths and weaknesses? (See Psalm 139 and recall the Westminster Shorter Catechism, Q/A 1.)

Select at least one weakness that is particularly distressing for you right now and write a wise prayer concerning it based upon what you have learned in these six chapters of study. Pray this prayer consistently during this week and record any resulting changes that you detect in your attitude and/or behavior.

Digging Deeper

1. Describe the controversy surrounding James 5:14–15. Before you studied this chapter, did you have an opinion as to what James is teaching in these verses? If so, what was it? If your opinion has changed after studying this chapter, explain both the change and how the change came about. Support your opinion with Scripture.

*"I believe there is scarcely
an error in doctrine
or a failure in applying Christian ethics
that cannot be traced finally
to imperfect and ignoble
thoughts about God."*

A. W. Tozer

Chapter Seven

Genuine Wisdom Exhorts

> *My brethren, if any among you strays from the truth, and one turns him back, let him know that he who turns a sinner from the error of his way will save his soul from death, and will cover a multitude of sins. (James 5:19–20)*

James's little epistle to suffering believers "dispersed abroad" (1:1) ends rather abruptly. There is no verbal signal—no *therefore* or *finally*—to alert us to the fact that he has completed his message. There are none of the usual "greetings" that close the majority of New Testament letters. And there is no obvious link between Elijah's exemplary prayers and James's last words. We definitely get the impression that something is missing. Has part of this letter been lost? Was James interrupted before he finished his thoughts? We simply don't know.

Of this, however, we can be certain: Every word of this letter that God wants us to read has been preserved (Deuteronomy 29:29). And it has been recorded precisely as He intended. Since God in His sovereignty has controlled the writing of Scripture (Romans 15:4; 2 Timothy 3:14–17; 2 Peter 1:20–21), we know that nothing "pertaining to life and godliness" (2 Peter 1:3) has slipped through the cracks. Therefore, wisdom suggests that we pay heed to what is here instead of engaging in vain speculations about what might be missing (Titus 3:9).

I think you will find, as I have, that pausing to ponder James's final sentence in humble submission to God's revelation yields a rich harvest of insight. Although at first glance we may detect only one last piece of advice for the good of the Church, upon closer inspection we unearth a bit more. These words also lay bare the humble *heart* of genuine wisdom while defending the boldness with which James had written.

Genuine wisdom is energized by its great love for others. It selflessly seeks after the highest good of a neighbor. Therefore, it does not hesitate to exhort the wayward. Genuine wisdom knows that straying from truth produces no good and that bold action is needed to turn wayward sinners from their errors. James was a man who possessed genuine wisdom and was thereby motivated to write the bold letter that we have studied. So far he has called us to adhere to God's truth in every situation of life; now he exhorts us to join him in the wise task of exhorting others.

The Value of Exhortation

James was an exhorter; that is, he concentrated upon calling people to live wisely by turning from their sinful ways to serve God in righteousness. James exhorted well because, like so many other writers of Scripture, he was a master of balancing conviction with comfort.

Exhortation in Scripture has to do with encouraging or, in other words, infusing courage or building strength to accomplish God's purposes.[1] It is a fascinating, multi-faceted concept that encompasses teaching, admonition, correction, and discipline as well as compassion, consolation, understanding, and motivation. Please note my emphasis on the word encompass, which means "to contain, surround, or encircle." Exhortation does not pick and choose among the activities listed; it wraps its powerful, loving arms around all of them!

Perhaps that is why so few Christians these days accept James's charge to exhort others biblically—and why the Church as a whole is lacking courage and strength. Exhortation is difficult; it requires patient endurance, knowledge of Scripture, and bold dependence on God. Most of us would simply rather not make such a great effort. Unfortunately, opting for ease doesn't benefit anyone. If we were all more adept at dispensing (and receiving!) fully orbed biblical exhortation, the Body of Christ would be built up mightily. But let's not sit around lamenting the problem when our time would be better spent examining James's example with the intent of accepting his challenge. How can his letter help us become better exhorters?

Do you remember the startling sentence with which James opened his letter? *Consider it all joy, my brethren, when you encounter various trials, knowing that the testing of your faith produces endurance* (1:2–3). That is a masterpiece of fully orbed biblical exhortation! And we can learn a great deal by analyzing it carefully. Before you read on, take a few minutes to note which "facets" of exhortation listed above you can spot in that sentence.

I'm sure that all of you grammar mavens recognized the imperative mood of the verb *consider*, which classifies the whole sentence as a command. Even if you aren't a grammar maven, you know that commands are associated with *admonitions and/or corrections.* They are issued in recognition of a need for change. It would be rather silly and pointless to command people to do what they are already doing!

Since commands call for a change of some sort, they demand obedience. And obedience depends upon teaching and discipline. Before James's readers will be able to effectively obey his command, they must be *taught* what, where, when, and how they are to obey; and they must exercise *discipline* (and perhaps even be disciplined) to put what they learn into practice.

But James is no heartless first sergeant, barking orders to people he doesn't care much about. He is writing to members of his spiritual family—and he loves them all dearly. Therefore, he not only commands them to do what is in their best interests but also consoles them with hope instead of frail sympathy. You may have noticed that James doesn't pat his readers figuratively on the back while murmuring, "Oh, you poor little things." Rather, he boldly presents them with his *understanding* of how their situation fits perfectly within God's purposes for them. They can and should consider trials as "all joy" because God uses them to build up the faith of His children.

Encouraging his distressed readers with this hopeful truth is an expression of James's wise compassion for them. It is important to know that compassion acts on another's behalf and thus moves beyond both sympathy (feelings of sorrow for another) and empathy (mental identification with someone else's situation). Sympathizing with people is good, and empathizing with them is better, but extending compassion toward them is best—and it is essential to exhortation because it fuels motivation. Whereas sympathy and empathy give hurting people a welcome shoulder to cry on, compassion helps them overcome their distress by pointing out the solution.

Of course, these three tools motivate best when they work together. When sympathy and empathy are unwisely extended, devoid of compassion, hurting people are often "encouraged" to sink into self-pity; and cold-hearted compassion comes across as so unloving and harsh that it typically motivates the distressed toward angry defensiveness. James, the master exhorter, skillfully wove all three together in the first words of his letter. His heartfelt identification with the plight of his readers is seen in the warm emotional phrase *my brethren*. And his wise compassion for them exudes from his bold, active directive to look at their circumstances from God's perspective.

Are you beginning to appreciate James's skill as an exhorter? If we had more time and energy, I'm sure we could analyze each sentence we've studied in his little letter just as we have his first one, but you can relax because we won't! What we will do instead is take a broad look at his overall exhortation to believers in Christ as a means of reviewing what we have learned in this *Faith at Work* series.

James's Epistle—One Long Exhortation

Yesterday I ran into a friend I hadn't seen in a couple of months, and one of the first things he asked me was, "How are you doing on James?" I told him that I was working on the last chapter and that I was truly excited to have seen the final sentence as both a summary and a defense of everything in the letter. My friend was intrigued and asked me to explain. What a great opportunity that was to sort out my thoughts for writing this section!

I told my friend some of what I've already told you-- that James 5:19–20 is where it is in this letter because God put it there, and that our job as wise readers of Scripture is to seek out His purpose for placing these words at the end of this letter. Since they describe the practice of exhortation and are included in a discussion of wise Christian living, we can deduce that exhortation is something wise Christians should practice. The fact that these words serve as the conclusion to James's letter could indicate that they summarize and defend his purpose and method of writing. And as I had thought back over the letter, I realized just how well they had done that.

The epistle of James is one long exhortation that ends with an exhortation to exhort others in the same way in which you have been exhorted because exhortation lies at the heart of wise Christian living. Whew! Did you get that? Let's go back and take a big-picture look at this letter so that we can better understand James's last words to his beloved, suffering brethren.

You remember, of course, that James wrote to believers who had been forced to flee from Jerusalem in the wake of intense persecution. (See Acts 8:1–4.) As they settled among strangers in foreign lands, they faced a variety of difficulties that produced a great deal of distress and discouragement. James, as the leader of the church in Jerusalem, had remained in residence there, but his heart was with the scattered believers. Since he could not assist them face to face, he wrote them this letter. And he chose as his primary means of assistance the strong tool of exhortation.

We have already seen how James's opening sentence sets the balanced convicting/comforting tone of the letter by lovingly directing his readers to look at their situation from God's perspective. The very next sentence assures them of the wisdom of that kind of behavior: It will make them "perfect and complete, lacking in nothing" (1:4).

James then begins teaching his readers how to acquire the wisdom they need to overcome distressing circumstances. They must wholeheartedly seek it from God, who will give it to them "generously and without reproach" (1: 5–8). They must rely solely on spiritual resources while persevering through trials, because the crown of life waits for those who do (vv. 9–12). They must never accuse God of using trials to tempt them to sin; rather, they must realize that trials degenerate from tests (designed by God to strengthen) to temptations (designed by Satan to weaken) when those enduring the trial are "carried away and enticed by [their] own lust" (vv. 13–15). They must guard against the deception of the world, the flesh, and the devil by remembering that all things come into their lives by God's design and under His control for the good dual purpose of His exaltation and their edification (vv. 17–18).

Now that they have learned these truths, readers must put them into practice. James tells them that righteousness does not result from responding in anger to God's sovereign providence, but rather from "putting aside all filthiness and all that remains of wickedness," from humbly receiving "the word implanted," and from proving themselves "doers of the word, and not merely hearers" (vv. 19–25). True religion, implanted by God's revealed truth, will be reflected in the way they treat others—in both word and deed (1:26–2:13; 3:1–12). That is because genuine faith works in the power of God. Faith without righteous works is a contradiction in terms, and is characteristic of demons (2:14–26).

Those whose faith works to accomplish God's purposes are truly wise. They walk righteously and at peace with one another because they submit humbly to God and resist the devil (3:13–4:10). Their habitual responses to the stresses and strains of daily living reflect a God-centered focus that both honors Him and fills up their joy (4:11–5:18). Since they have both learned and applied what they have been taught, their next step is to exhort (that is, to encourage by teaching, admonishing, correcting, disciplining, extending compassion, consoling, understanding, and motivating) their brothers and sisters to come and do likewise (5:19–20).

From Exhorted to Exhorter

Even though James's directive is clear, most Christians I know shy away (or even recoil!) from exhorting others. When I ask them why, they usually mumble something about "being tolerant of those who hold different opinions" or declare that they just aren't "qualified" to do such a thing. Now at first blush, those answers may seem very loving and humble—but let's think for a moment about whether they really are so.

Do we love others by tolerating, ignoring, or even encouraging their descent into error? Do we act in humility by coming up with excuses for not doing what God clearly tells us to do in His Word? Scripture answers "No" to both questions. James himself tells us that taking action to turn "a sinner from the error of his way will save his soul from death, and will cover a multitude of sins" (5:19). Doesn't such behavior reflect the highest possible love for another? And since Paul says that every word of the Bible has been recorded for our instruction in righteousness and to give us hope (2 Timothy 3:16–17; Romans 15:4), shouldn't we follow James's exhortative example? We must answer "Yes" to both questions.

Paul echoes James's teaching that wise Christian living includes exhortation when he instructs the Galatians, "Brethren, even if a man is caught in any trespass, you who are spiritual, restore such a one in a spirit of gentleness; each one looking to yourself, lest you too be tempted" (Galatians 6:1). Those who are spiritual are those who read and apply God's truth in their lives. In the words of our Savior, they are those who have taken the log out their eye so that they can see clearly to take the speck out of the eye of a wayward brother or sister (Matthew 7:2–5).

The Church of Jesus Christ will be built up and strengthened when its individual members (that's you and I!) listen to God and do what He says. We can do that without fear because His commands are not burdensome. He is our loving Father, who loves us perfectly and knows what we need. Therefore, He exhorts us in His Word, through writers like James, to live wisely in humble dependence upon Him. Obeying such exhortation glorifies God and enhances our joy as we "work out our salvation" in pursuit of His purposes in our daily lives.

But our new life in Christ cannot be worked out effectively in isolation from the rest of the family. James has both exemplified for us and exhorted us to accept the essential task of encouraging others just as we have been encouraged. Will we make excuses—or do what he says? Will we prove ourselves doers of the word—or merely hearers? Will Christ's Church increase in courage and strength because we have heeded James's exhortation—or will it grow more fearful and weak because we have ignored him?

I say, let's join together in renewed commitment to walk worthy of our high calling in Christ by living wisely in the light of God's revealed truth!

---

1   Lawrence O. Richards, *Expository Dictionary of Bible Words*, s. v. "encourage." Grand Rapids: Regency Reference Library, 1985.

Review Questions

1. In your own words, describe *exhortation*. Then briefly explain exhortation's place in wise Christian living.

2. Explain how James's final sentence can be seen as (1) good advice for the Church, (2) the "purpose statement" of his letter, and (3) a defense of the boldness with which he wrote. (NOTE: A "purpose statement" reveals the author's reason[s] for writing. See Lesson 4 of my Light for Your Path study, *Turning on the Light*, for more information about purpose statements.)

3. How does good, biblical exhortation balance conviction with comfort? Why do you think it is important to balance conviction with comfort?

4. Describe how James balances conviction with comfort in the opening sentence of his letter (1:2–3) as he addresses believers who have been dispersed abroad.

5. Distinguish between sympathy, empathy, and compassion. Which of these tools is most effective in motivating believers to apply scriptural truth in their lives? Explain your answer.

6. Read through the book of James and record phrases and sentences that exhort believers in the following ways. (NOTE: If you are unsure of the meanings of the following words, look them up in a dictionary before you begin. Also be aware that many phrases and sentences in the book of James can be placed reasonably in more than one category.)

Teaching:

Admonition:

Correction:

Discipline:

Compassion:

Consolation:

Understanding:

Motivation:

7. How does shying away or recoiling from exhortation reveal a lack of love and humility on the part of a believer?

Applying the Word

1. Read through the book of James once again and then look over your answer to Review Question 6. Prayerfully consider which of the many exhortations contained in this epistle convict you regarding your walk with the Lord. List at least three of those below. Then list the exhortations that you find most comforting.

   Regarding the areas in which you have been convicted, what does the book of James teach you to do? How does it admonish and correct you? How must you exercise self-discipline in these areas? What kind of discipline may you expect from God if you take no action in these areas?

Regarding the areas in which you have been comforted, how has James acted compassionately toward you? How has he consoled you? How has he indicated that he understands your situation? In what ways has he motivated you to act and think differently?

Describe at least three ways in which your life will change (or has changed already) as a result of having studied the book of James.

Digging Deeper

1. A. W. Tozer said, "I believe there is scarcely an error in doctrine or a failure in applying Christian ethics that cannot be traced finally to imperfect and ignoble thoughts about God." Would James have agreed with Tozer? Explain your answer thoroughly.

Recommended Reading

Jay Adams, *A Thirst for Wholeness*. Wheaton, Ill.: Victor Books, 1988.

John Blanchard, *Truth for Life: A Devotional Commentary on the Epistle of James*. Durham, England: Evangelical Press, 1986.

Robert Bolton, *General Directions for a Comfortable Walking with God*. Originally published, 1626; reprint, Religious Tract Society, 1837; reprint, Ligonier, Penn.: Soli Deo Gloria Publications, 1991.

Jerry Bridges, *Transforming Grace: Living Confidently in God's Unfailing Love*. Colorado Springs: Navpress, 1991.

The Joy of Fearing God. Colorado Springs: WaterBrook Press, 1997.

D. Edmond Hiebert, *James*. Chicago: Moody Press, 1979, 1992. (original title: *The Epistle of James*).

J. Gresham Machen, *The Christian View of Man*. Carlisle, PA: The Banner of Truth Trust, 1984 (first published: 1937)

John Murray, *Principles of Conduct*. Grand Rapids: Wm. B. Eerdmans Publishing, 1957.

John Piper, *Desiring God: Meditations of a Christian Hedonist.* Sisters, Ore.: Multnomah Books, 1986, 1996

Carol J. Ruvolo, *Before the Throne of God: Focus on Prayer.* Phillipsburg, N.J.: P & R Publishing, 1999. (The Light for Your Path Series)

J. C. Ryle, *Practical Religion.* Carlisle, PA: The Banner of Truth Trust, 1998. (first published: 1878)

Joni Eareckson Tada and Steven Estes, *When God Weeps: Why Our Sufferings Matter to the Almighty.* Grand Rapids: Zondervan Publishing House, 1997.

Appendix A

What Must I Do to Be Saved?

A strange sound drifted through the Philippian jail as midnight approached. It was the sound of human voices—but not the expected groans of the two men who earlier had been beaten with rods and fastened in stocks. Rather, the peaceful singing of praises to their God floated through the cells.

While the other prisoners quietly listened to them, the jailer dozed off, content with the bizarre calm generated by these two preachers, who had stirred so much commotion in the city just hours before.

Suddenly a deafening roar filled the prison, and the ground began to shake violently. Sturdy doors convulsed and popped open. Chains snapped and fell at prisoners' feet. Startled into full wakefulness, the jailer stared, horrified, at the wide-open doors that guaranteed his prisoners' escape—and his own death. Under Roman law, jailers paid with their lives when prisoners escaped. Resolutely, he drew his sword, thinking it better to die by his own hand than by Roman execution.

"Stop! Don't harm yourself—we are all here!" a voice boomed from the darkened inner cell. The jailer called for lights and was astonished to discover his prisoners standing quietly amid their broken chains. Trembling with fear, he rushed in and fell at the feet of the two preachers. As soon as he was able, he led them out of the ruined prison and asked in utter astonishment, "Sirs, What must I do to be saved?"

In the entire history of the world, no one has ever asked a more important question. The jailer's words that day may well have been motivated by his critical physical need, but the response of Paul and Silas addressed his even more critical spiritual need: "Believe in the Lord Jesus, and you shall be saved, you and your household."[1]

If you have never "believed in the Lord Jesus," your spiritual need, just like the jailer's, is critical. As long as your life is stained with sin, God cannot receive you into His presence. The Bible says that sin has placed a separation between you and God (Isaiah 59:2). It goes on to say that your nature has been so permeated by sin that you no longer have any desire to serve and obey God (Romans 3:10–12); therefore, you are not likely to recognize or care that a separation exists. Your situation is truly desperate because those who are separated from God will spend eternity in hell.

Since your sinful nature is unresponsive to God, the only way you can be saved from your desperate situation is for God to take the initiative. And this He has done! Even though all men and women deserve the punishment of hell because of their sin, God's love has prompted Him to save some who will serve Him in obedience. He did this by sending His Son, the Lord Jesus Christ, to remove the barrier of sin between God and His chosen ones (Colossians 2:13–14).

What is there about Jesus that enables Him to do this? First of all, He is God. While He was on earth He said, "He who has seen Me has seen the Father" (John 14:9) and "I and the Father are one" (John 10:30). Because He said these things, you must conclude one of three things about His true identity: (1) He was a lunatic who believed he was God when he really wasn't; (2) He was a liar who was willing to die a hideous death for what he knew was a lie; or (3) His words are true and He is God.

Lunatics don't live the way Jesus did, and liars don't die the way He did; so if the Bible's account of Jesus' life and words is true, you can be sure He *is* God.

Since Jesus is God, He is perfectly righteous and holy. God's perfect righteousness and holiness demands that sin be punished (Ezekiel 18:4), and Jesus' perfect righteousness and holiness qualified Him to bear the punishment for the sins of those who will be saved (Romans 6:23). Jesus is the only person who never committed a sin; therefore, the punishment He bore when He died on the cross could be accepted by God as satisfaction of His justice in regard to the sins of others.

If someone you love commits a crime and is sentenced to die, you may offer to die in his place. However, if you also have committed crimes worthy of death, your death cannot satisfy the law's demands for your crimes *and* your loved one's. You can die in his place only if you are innocent of any wrongdoing.

Since Jesus lived a perfect life, God's justice could be satisfied by allowing Him to die for the sins of those who will be saved. Because God is perfectly righteous and holy, He could not act in love at the expense of justice. By sending Jesus to die, God demonstrated His love *by acting to satisfy His own justice* (Romans 3:26).

Jesus did more than die, however; He also rose from the dead. By raising Jesus from the dead, God declared that He had accepted Jesus' death in the place of those who will be saved. Because Jesus lives eternally with God, those for whom Jesus died can be assured that they also will spend eternity in heaven (John 14:1–3). The separation of sin has been removed!

Ah, but the all-important question remains unanswered: What must *you do* to be saved? If God has sent His Son into the world for sinners, and Jesus Christ died in their place, what is left for you to do? You must respond in faith to what God has done. This is what Paul meant when he told the jailer, "Believe in the Lord Jesus, and you shall be saved."

Believing in the Lord Jesus demands three responses from you: (1) an understanding of the facts regarding your hopeless sinful condition and God's action to remove the sin barrier that separates you from Him; (2) acceptance of those facts as true and applicable to you; and (3) a willingness to trust and depend upon God to save you from sin. This involves willingly placing yourself under His authority and acknowledging His sovereign right to rule over you.

But, you say, how can I do this if sin has eliminated my ability to know and appreciate God's work on my behalf? Rest assured that if you desire to have the sin barrier that separates you from God removed, He already is working to change your natural inability to respond. He is extending His gracious offer of salvation to you and will give you the faith to receive it.

If you believe that God is working to call you to Himself, read the words He has written to you in the Bible (perhaps beginning with the book of John in the New Testament) and pray that His Holy Spirit will help you understand what is written there. Continue to read and pray until you are ready to *repent*—that is, to turn away from sin and commit yourself to serving God.

Is there any other way you can be saved? God Himself says no, there is not. The Bible He wrote says that Jesus is the only way in which the sin barrier between you and God can be removed (John 14:6; Acts 4:12). He is your hope, and He is your *only* hope.

If you have questions or need any help in this matter, please write to The Evangelism Team, Providence Presbyterian Church, P. O. Box 14651, Albuquerque, NM 87191, before the day is over. God has said in His Bible that a day of judgment is coming, and after that day no one will be saved (Acts 17:30–31; 2 Thessalonians 1:7–9). The time to act is now.

---

[1] For a full biblical account of this event, see Acts 16:11–40.

Appendix B

What Is the Reformed Faith?

The term *the Reformed Faith*[1] can be defined as a theology that describes and explains the sovereign God's revelation of His actions in history to glorify Himself by redeeming selected men and women from the just consequences of their self-inflicted depravity.

It is first and foremost *theology* (the study of God), not *anthropology* (the study of man). Reformed thinking concentrates on developing a true knowledge of God that serves as the necessary context for all other knowledge. It affirms that the created world, including humanity itself, cannot be accurately understood apart from its relationship with the Creator.

The Reformed Faith describes and explains God's revelation of Himself and His actions to humanity; it does not consist of people's attempts to define God as they wish. The Reformed Faith asserts that God has revealed Himself in two distinct ways: He reveals His existence, wisdom, and power through the created universe—a process known as *natural revelation* (Romans 1:18–32); and He reveals His requirements and plans for mankind through His written Word, the Bible—a process known as *special revelation* (2 Timothy 3:16–17).

Reformed theologians uphold the Bible as the inspired, infallible, inerrant, authoritative, and fully sufficient communication of truth from God to humanity. When they call the Bible *inspired*, they mean that the Bible was actually written by God through the agency of human authorship in a miraculous way that preserved the thoughts of God from the taint of human sinfulness (2 Peter 1:20–21). When they call the Bible *infallible*, they mean that it is *incapable* of error. When they call it *inerrant*, they mean that the Bible, *in actual fact*, contains no errors. The Bible is authoritative because it comes from God, whose authority over His creation is absolute (Isaiah 46:9–10). And it is completely sufficient because it contains everything necessary for us to know and live according to God's requirements (2 Peter 1:3–4).

By studying God's revelation of Himself and His work, Reformed theologians have learned two foundational truths that structure their thinking about God's relationship with human beings: God is absolutely sovereign, and people are totally depraved.[2]

Reformed thought affirms that God, by definition, is absolutely sovereign—that is, He controls and superintends every circumstance of life, either by direct miraculous intervention or by the ordinary outworking of His providence. Reformed theologians understand that a "god" who is not sovereign cannot be God because his power would not be absolute. Since the Reformed Faith accepts the Bible's teaching regarding the sovereignty of God, it denies that anything occurs outside of God's control.

The Reformed Faith affirms the biblical teaching that Adam was created with the ability to sin and that he chose to sin by disobeying a clear command of God (Genesis 3:1–7).

Choosing to sin changed basic human nature and left us unable not to sin—or *totally depraved*. Total depravity does not mean that all people are as bad as they possibly could be, but that every facet of their character is tainted with sin, leaving them incapable and undesirous of fellowship with God. The Reformed Faith denies that totally depraved men and women have any ability to seek after or submit to God of their own free will. Left to themselves, totally depraved men and women will remain out of fellowship with God for all eternity.

The only way for any of these men and women to have their fellowship with God restored is for God Himself to take the initiative. And the Bible declares that He has graciously chosen to do so (John 14:16). *For His own glory*, He has chosen some of those depraved men and women to live in fellowship with Him. His choice is determined by His own good pleasure and not by any virtue in the ones He has chosen. For this reason, *grace* is defined in Reformed thought as "unmerited favor."

God accomplished the salvation of His chosen ones by sending His Son, the Lord Jesus Christ, to bear God's righteous wrath against sin so that He could forgive those He had chosen. Even though Christ's work was perfect and complete, its effectiveness is limited to those who are chosen by God for salvation. Christ would not have been required to suffer any more or any less had a different number been chosen for redemption, but the benefit of His suffering is applied only to those who are called by God to believe in Him. And all those who are effectually called by God eventually will believe and be saved, even though they may resist for a time (John 6:37). They cannot forfeit the salvation they have received (John 10:27–30; Romans 8:31–39).

Reformed thought affirms the clear teaching of the Bible that salvation is by faith alone through Christ alone (John 14:6; Acts 4:12; Ephesians 2:8–9) and that human works play no part in salvation although they are generated by it (Ephesians 2:10). Salvation transforms a person's nature, giving him or her the ability and the desire to serve and obey God. The unresponsive heart of stone is changed into a sensitive heart of flesh that responds readily to God's voice (Ezekiel 36:25–27) and desires to glorify Him out of gratitude for the indescribable gift of salvation.

Reformed thought affirms that God works in history to redeem His chosen ones through a series of covenants. These covenants define His Law, assess penalties for breaking His Law, and provide for the imputation of Jesus' vicarious fulfillment of God's requirements to those God intends to redeem.[3]

The Reformed Faith affirms that we were created and exist solely to glorify God, and it denies that God exists to serve us. It affirms that God acts to glorify Himself by putting His attributes on display and that His self-glorifying actions are thoroughly righteous since He is the only Being in creation worthy of glorification. It denies that God is motivated to act primarily by man's needs; rather, it affirms that all of God's actions are motivated primarily for His own glory.

The Reformed Faith emerged as a distinct belief system during the sixteenth and seventeenth centuries when men like Luther, Calvin, Zwingli, and Knox fought against the Roman Catholic Church to restore Christian doctrine to biblical truth. These men were labeled Reformers, but they would have been better labeled Restorers since their goal was to correct abuses and distortions of Christianity that were rampant in the established Roman church. Reformed thinkers since their day have sought to align their own understanding of God and His actions in history as closely as possible to His revealed truth.

[1] This brief overview of basic Reformed beliefs is not intended to be a full explanation of or apologetic for the Reformed Faith. For a more detailed description and analysis of the Reformed Faith see: R. C. Sproul, Grace Unknown (Grand Rapids: Baker Books, 1997); Loraine Boettner, The Reformed Faith (Phillipsburg, N.J.: Presbyterian and Reformed, 1983); Back to Basics: Rediscovering the Richness of the Reformed Faith, ed. David G. Hagopian (Phillipsburg, N.J.: P & R Publishing, 1996); The Westminster Confession of Faith (with its accompanying Catechisms); or the theological writings of John Calvin, B. B. Warfield, Charles Hodge, and Louis Berkhof.

[2] Both of these truths are taught throughout the pages of Scripture; however, the sovereignty of God can be seen very clearly in Isaiah 40–60 and in Job 38–42, while the total depravity of man is described quite graphically in Romans 3:10–18.

[3] An excellent discussion of these covenants is contained in Chapter 5 of R. C. Sproul, Grace Unknown.

The Purpose of Deo Volente Publishing

"And do not be conformed to this world,
but be transformed by the renewing of your mind,
that you may prove what is that good and
acceptable and perfect will of God"
Romans 12:2 (NKJV)

Deo Volente Publishing exists to help make the exhortation of Romans 12:2 a living, daily reality in the believer's life.

Our goal is:
- to edify believers in Christ,
- to encourage non-conformity to the world's standards,
- to exhort believers to live radically transformed lives that reflect the knowledge, enjoyment and practice of what is good, acceptable, and perfect in God's sight.

We will endeavor to meet our goal by publishing material that:
- is consistently Reformed in theology,
- is intensely practical for a daily Christian walk,
- and encourages holy living in every aspect of life through the reforming power of God's Word.

DEO VOLENTE

PUBLISHING

P.O. BOX 4847
LOS ALAMOS, NM 87544